Symbols of
Native America

About this book:
In today's world, which is so radically different from the world in which we originated, there is a growing longing to become closer to nature. This longing is, for example, expressed in the interest that many people today show toward Native Americans, as they seem to epitomize a life at one with nature. This harmony is expressed through the rituals of the different Native American tribes—rituals of which we often have knowledge only through symbols. These symbols are used as ornaments and to decorate jewelry, textiles, and accessories. Only a few people actually know the meaning of these symbols. But it is this meaning that transforms an ornament into a symbol, because, for the beholder, it represents a ritual and thus is given significance. In this book, you will find about three hundred Native American symbols that are reintroduced in their original context and can, therefore, bring us a little closer to our Earth.

About the author:
Heike Owusu gained a spiritual insight into the world from an early age—something that both her family and her peers were unable to relate to. When her life was threatened by a severe illness, she managed to recover with the help of meditation, relaxation, and a self-healing method she developed herself. Her marriage to a Ghanaian husband increased her already great desire to learn about primitive tribes, including their knowledge and mythology. All this helped her to release her artistic potential so that today she passes her knowledge on in cosmic pictures, in illustrations, and through writing.

Symbols of Native America

Heike Owusu

Sterling Publishing Co., Inc.
New York

Library of Congress Cataloging-in-Publication Data

Owusu, Heike
   [Symbole der Indianer Nordamerikas. English]
   Symbols of native America / by Heikie Owusu.
   p. cm
   Originally published : Symbole der Indianer Nordamerikas.
Darmstadt : Schiner Verlag, c1997.
   Includes index.
   ISBN 0-8069-6347-6
   1. Indianns of North America—Rites and ceremonies. 2. Indians of North
America—Religion. 3. Signs and symbols—North America. 4. Symbolism
in art—North America. I. Title.
E98.R5309813 1999
302.2'223'08997—dc21   98-51478
                                         CIP

10 9 8 7 6 5

Published by Sterling Publishing Co., Inc.
387 Park Avenue South, New York, N.Y. 10016
Originally published in Germany by Schirner Verlag, Darmstadt
under the title *Symbole der Indianer Nordamerikas*
© 1997 by Schirner Verlag, Darmstadt
English translation © 1999 by Sterling Publishing Co., Inc.
Distributed in Canada by Sterling Publishing
c/o Canadian Manda Group, 165 Dufferin Street
Toronto, Ontario, Canada M6K 3H6
Distributed in Great Britain by Chrysalis Books Group PLC
The Chrysalis Building, Bramley Road, London, W10 6SP, England
Distributed in Australia by Capricorn Link (Australia) Pty. Ltd.
P.O. Box 704, Windsor, NSW 2756, Australia
Manufactured in the United States of America
All rights reserved

Sterling ISBN 0-8069-6347-6

Contents

Preface

This book aims to provide a detailed overview of the rich symbolism used by the natives of North America. Sadly, due to the alienation from their culture, which occurred as a result of the European conquest of the American continent, Native Americans have forgotten a great deal of the meaning and spiritual knowledge that is part of their culture. What makes matters more difficult is the fact that this community is made up of a vast number of different tribes, who not only speak different languages but also have different views of the world. This book cannot treat in detail those isolated cultures that differ greatly from the other Native American tribes.

All native inhabitants of the North American continent strive to improve their relationship with Mother Earth and her creatures. The spiritual goal of all Native American religions is to live in harmony with the universe. To attain this goal, tribes use numerous rituals and symbols that have their origins in different traditions. These rituals and symbols are employed during important celebrations, family events, and in everyday life, because, for the Native American, everything is animated and full of deep symbolism—even the simplest items of everyday use. As a result, all objects and beings that surround the individual deserve one's attention and respect.

Whenever this book mentions "medicine," it refers to all those powers that have a positive influence on man and improve his relationship with all living creatures. These creatures can be animals, plants, stones, or even man-made items.

At a time when people have moved so far away from nature, it seems even more important that we aim to develop a loving relationship with all beings and give them our respect—the animal people, the standing people (trees), the stone people, and the star people.

7

1

Simple Symbols

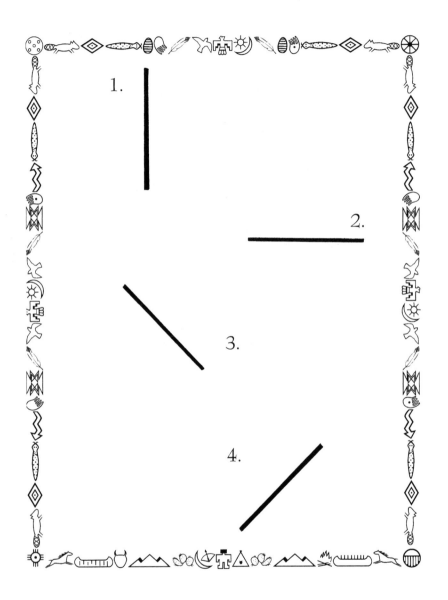

1.

2.

3.

4.

Straight Lines

A straight, vertical line (Fig. 1) represents immediate spiritual power. It shows the upward movement of a spiritual path through life. Furthermore, it represents the Earth spirit.

A horizontal line (Fig. 2) represents the fertility and movement of the Earth. It is a symbol of willpower and may refer to somebody with a close relationship to the Earth.

A line that slants to the left (Fig. 3) allows a person to integrate the experiences and gifts of learning into his own being.

A line that slants to the right (Fig. 4) leads magnetic forces into a person's being.

If both slanted lines appear simultaneously, they refer to a person who attains the power of leadership by living as an example to others.

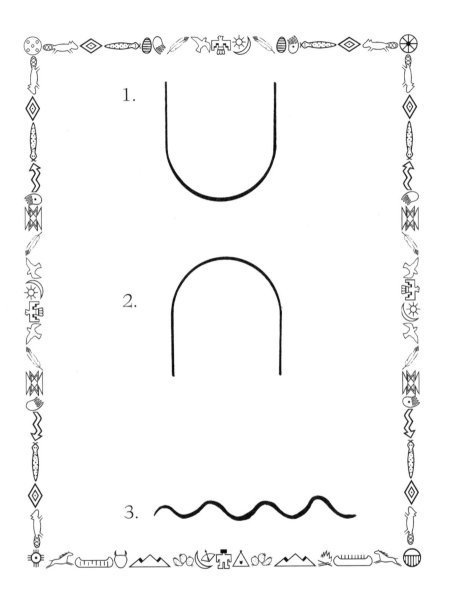

1.

2.

3.

Curved Lines

The U symbol (Fig. 1) means old wounds will be healed through gratitude. The sign refers to healing through spiritual growth.

The upside-down U symbol (Fig. 2) refers to teachings that are suited to create a solid foundation from which a person can grow. It represents the power of influence.

A wavy line (Fig. 3) represents the energy that builds matter. This refers to both the application of physical energy and spiritual energy.

1.

2.

3.

Crossed-line Symbols

The simple X (Fig. 1) represents a man, the male power, and masculinity. It shows the power of being able to put an idea into practice.

If X has a small circle above it (Fig. 2), it represents a woman and the female power. It is the nurturing principle and also means compassion.

A cross made up of a horizontal and a vertical line (Fig. 3) indicates steadfastness. It is a combination of Earth (vertical) and sky (horizontal).

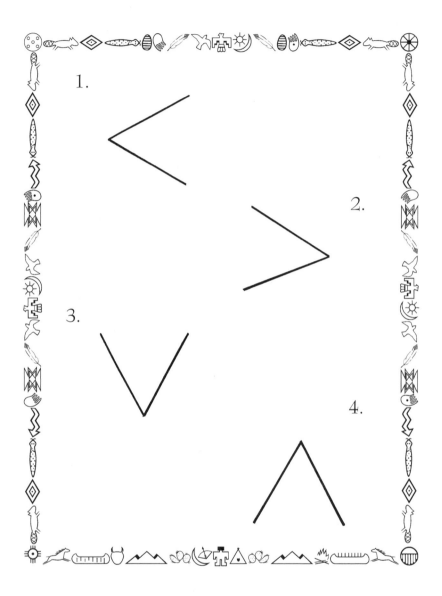

1.

2.

3.

4.

V Shapes

A V pointing to the left (Fig. 1) signifies a respectful attitude. It indicates a person's ability to accept responsibility and respond.

A V pointing to the right (Fig. 2) represents the power of grateful acceptance. It also stands for the acceptance of truth.

An upright V (Fig. 3) may signify a creative idea. It may also represent the power of the spirit with its ability to deliberate, think independently, and use its intelligence positively. This is the holy point of view.

An upside-down V (Fig. 4) represents the power of truth. If it refers to a person, it may mean that he is not easily fooled by half-truths or distracted by an eloquent tongue.

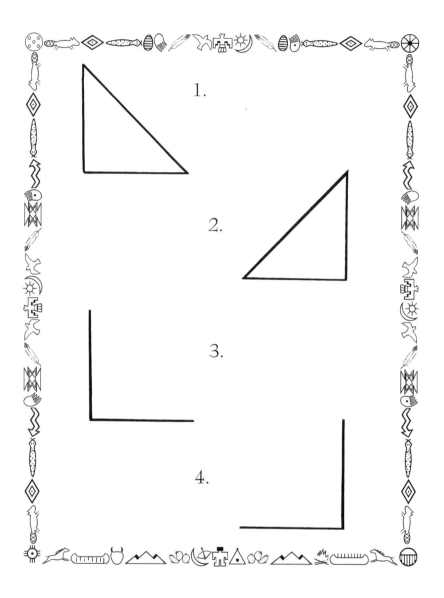

1.

2.

3.

4.

Right Triangles and Angles

A right-angled triangle with its hypotenuse to the right (Fig. 1) expresses the strength of a conscious existence and self-confidence. It also stands for physical power.

A right-angled triangle with its hypotenuse to the left (Fig. 2) symbolizes the development of talents or divine gifts and represents the energy of having an incentive.

A right angle open to the right (Fig. 3) calls us to honor truth and wisdom. It represents learning.

A right angle open to the left (Fig. 4) is a sign of trust and willingness to help. It embodies the power of work directed toward the highest goal.

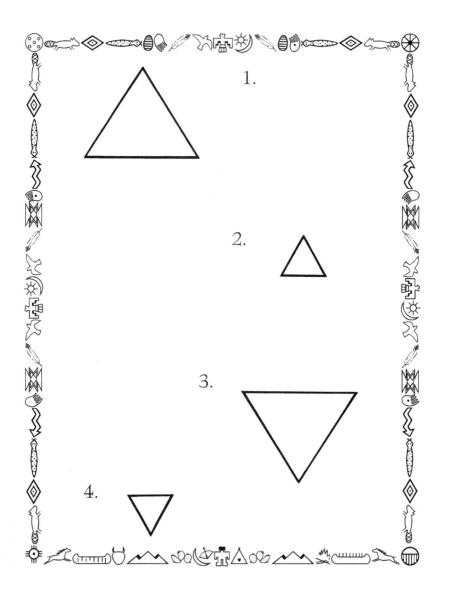

1.

2.

3.

4.

Equilateral Triangles

A large equilateral triangle that points upward (Fig. 1) is a sign of wisdom, inner knowledge, equality, and sensitivity. All points of view and all events are united in the highest, divine point.

A small equilateral triangle (Fig. 2) describes the power of creativity. It symbolizes hidden talents that should be brought to life and developed.

A large equilateral triangle that points downward (Fig. 3) stands for the trust in divine guidance and the recognition of the divine point of view. It points out that we ourselves are the cause of everything that happens to us.

A small upside-down equilateral triangle (Fig. 4) represents the power of inspiration and spiritualism. It also marks a person who can inspire others.

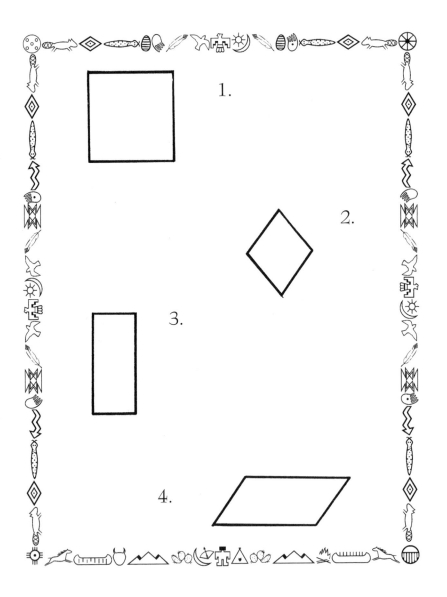

Quadrilateral Shapes

A square (Fig. 1) expresses steadfastness and reliability. It offers organized protection. Everything is built on solid foundations.

A diamond shape (Fig. 2) represents the protective force of the wind. It stands for the four stages of learning in a person's life. As a symbol of life, it represents eternal equality, unity, and freedom from fear.

An upright rectangle (Fig. 3) represents concentration on one thing alone. If it refers to a person, it means that the person concerned prefers to work alone or is a loner.

A parallelogram (Fig. 4) represents the power to move up through the ability to learn and accept new ideas. If it tilts to the left, it indicates the realization of goals. If it tilts to the right, it indicates that someone will receive enlightenment.

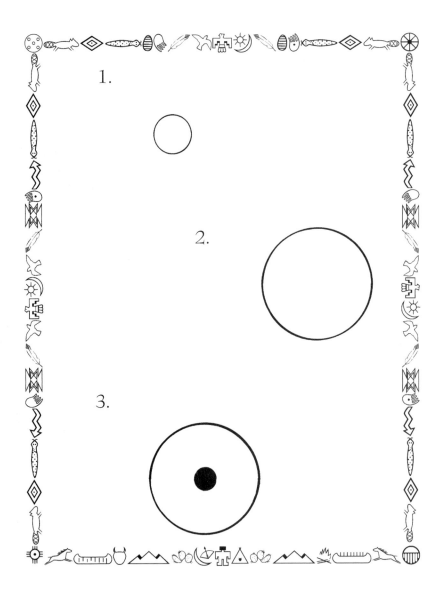

1.

2.

3.

Circles

A small circle (Fig. 1) represents the Moon, the color white, and the forces of change and growth.

A perfect large circle (Fig. 2) symbolizes the spirit in its original form. Therefore, on the one hand, it can represent the Sun, the male, the power of love, and the color yellow; on the other hand, it can also represent the female, the family, and sensitivity.

A dot in the center of a circle (Fig. 3) stands for the seed of the male principle while the circle represents the female principle, which nurtures the seed. This symbol can also indicate a union, pact, or marriage.

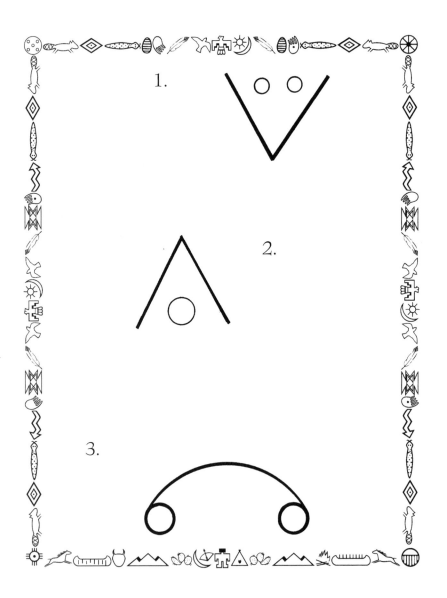

1.

2.

3.

Combined Symbols

An upright V containing two small circles (Fig. 1) represents the search for truth and the secrets of life.

A upside-down V that encloses a small circle (Fig. 2) indicates eloquence, but it can also stand for a person who talks too much.

A curve that connects two small circles (Fig. 3) indicates a certain dependence on material things. This symbol can be used to describe somebody who is a collector or somebody who should maybe learn the art of giving.

1.

2.

3.

Sun-shaped Symbols

Figure 1 shows a circle with straight lines that represent the rays of the Sun. The twelve rays indicate that the symbol stands for a medicine wheel with the twelve directions of love and happiness.

Figure 2 shows a Sun in motion that has seven rays. It represents the seven energy centers of a human being and the ability for the centers to develop. This symbol encourages talents and healing, and stands for a peace-loving person.

The Sun in Figure 3 is represented by a dot from which four rays emerge: to the North, South, East, and West. It, therefore, represents spiritual consciousness and consideration. The latter implies that the development of others should be respected without trying to influence them.

2

Symbols Common to Different Tribes

1.

2.

3.

Common symbols of spiritual healing

Kokopelli (Kókopilau): The Hunchbacked Flute Player

This symbol is shared by many tribes and can be found everywhere etched into rock—from Hopi territory in the Southwest via the southern tip of America to the far North of Canada.

The grasshopper *máhu* is known as the hunchbacked flute player. As a *kachina* (see page 53), it received the name of *kókopilau* because of its wooden appearance (*koko* = wood and *pilau* = hump).

In the beginning, when people started on their treks, they were accompanied by two insect-beings (*máhu*). After they had climbed a high mountain, they encountered a big eagle there. One of the *máhu* spoke for the people and asked the eagle whether it had been living there for a long time and whether it would allow the people to settle here. The eagle answered that it had been in this country since the creation of the fourth world and that it had to test them first before it could allow them to stay in this country.

After a difficult test, which they passed, the eagle shot an arrow through the first *máhu*'s body. Immediately, the *máhu* began to play a sweet, tender melody on its flute. After the eagle shot another arrow through a second *máhu*, who then played even sweeter tunes on its flute, the eagle recognized their power: The positive vibrations of their music strengthened their spirits, which then healed their injured bodies. With this realization, the eagle granted them permission to settle in his country.

Ever since, people have sung to their sick children, having discovered the healing powers of music.

Figure 1: Blue Flute. Figure 2: Gray Flute. Figure 3: Spirit or *kachina*.

33

*Earth symbols of different tribes asking for protection
from the Four Corners of the Earth*

Symbols of the Earth (1)

Since Native American thinking does not regard the shapes of circle, square, diamond, and rectangle as mutually exclusive, all four can be found as symbols representing the Earth. The square shape is usually predominant with the tribes of the forests, canyons, and mountains. In the wide and open plains, the circular shape developed, since there the horizon appears to be a circular line.

The symbol of honor of the Omaha (Fig. 1) can mostly be found as a picture on gourd rattles. The painted ring symbolizes the boundary of the sky and horizon; the four lines pointing outward from the ring represent the "four paths of the wind," the four directions from which the people will receive help.

Figure 2 represents the motif at the center of the symbol of honor of the Osage. It shows the Earth with its four cardinal points from which the winds blow consistently toward the center.

A typical ornament of feather headdresses (Fig. 3) can often be found among the tribes of the prairie. Traditionally, this design was embroidered on buffalo blankets with birds' feathers. Again, it represents the Earth with its four cardinal points.

The miniature of the Earth (Fig. 4), which is found sewn on the back of leather tepees, is a traditional symbol of the Arapaho. Its alternating concentric circles of yellow and black represent the growing original Earth, which started out small but came to its present size as the Whirlwind Woman continually circled it.

The box pattern (Fig. 5) shows a characteristic decoration that can be seen on the buffalo cloaks of Sioux women. It represents one of the Earth's microcosms. The four extrusions at the top describe the four winds; the other signs show the abundance and diversity of the Earth. The box pattern also symbolizes geographical contents, but their meanings have mostly been lost through the passage of time.

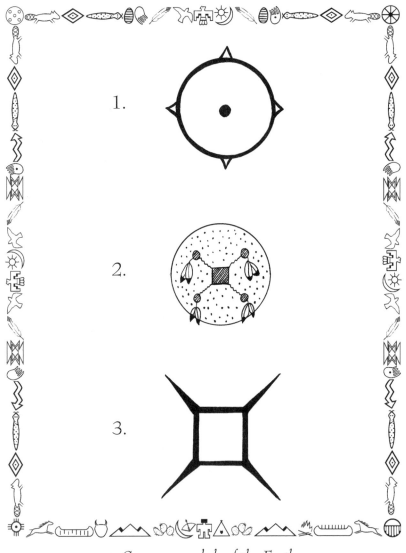

1.

2.

3.

Common symbols of the Earth

Symbols of the Earth (2)

Figure 1 shows a symbol shared by different tribes that appears again and again in slight variations. The symbol shown here is from the Lenape-Algonquin. It describes the four-cornered Earth and simultaneously also the "first existing being," the highest god. The four corners of the Earth stand for the four cardinal points, the four winds, the four seasons, the four elements, and the four human races.

The first song of the *Walam Olum*, the tribe's chronicle, says about the symbol of the four-cornered Earth: *"Kitanitowit* was the first existing being—above all, eternal, and invisible." The circle alone means "spirit." Only after the four corners are added is the symbol transformed to represent the "Great Spirit."

The shield in Figure 2 shows the four-cornered Earth in front of a blue sky, suspended by the four cardinal points from which feathers are hung. This is a decoration on a shield of the Dakota. Again, it emphasizes that the Native American view sees the highest god (manitu), the universe, and the Earth as representing one unit.

Figure 3 shows the *umane* (holy symbol) of the Sioux as a symbol of the Earth and four winds that blow from the four cardinal points toward the center. Native American thinking regards a square and a circle as having the same meaning. Therefore, both round and square shapes are representative of the Earth.

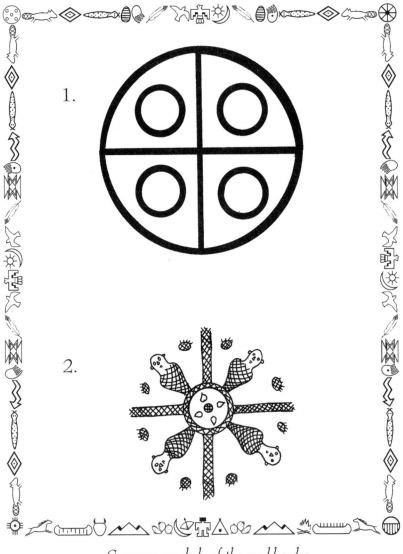

1.

2.

Common symbols of the world order

Symbols of the World

Figure 1 shows the world as seen by the Hopi in Arizona. The four end-points of the cosmic cross correspond to the outermost points on the visible horizon where the Sun passes on its way through the year. These are the points of solstice and equinox. Furthermore, they represent the cardinal points of East, West, North, and South—i.e., the points of intersection with the cosmic cross. The four circles represent the four nations, or races, which came into the world to keep it in balance.

The symbol in Figure 2 has a comparable meaning. It is a rendering by the Ojibwa in Minnesota and shows the Earth at the beginning of time when the four races came into the world and settled in the areas to which they were assigned, thus, maintaining the world order.

A symbol of life and fertility

The Tree of Life

The tree of life is a shared symbol that can be found in slightly altered forms with all tribes of North, Central, and South America. It represents the very first tree and the same powers are attributed to it everywhere: It causes rain to fall, plants to be reborn every spring, and it brings about the fertility of the Earth and of women.

The world tree shown on the opposite page is a depiction by the Omaha tribe. During a ritual with cosmic elements, a cotton tree would be felled and its leaves removed. It would then be carried to the settlement where two men would paint it with red and black rings. These rings represent day and night, thunder and death, sky and Earth—in short, all those powers that revive and preserve. The tree would then be erected at the center of the settlement, which is the square where the ritual dances took place.

The tree of life, as it is depicted here or in a similar fashion, is a tradition among many tribes that goes back 1000 years or more.

3

The Southwest

APACHE, HOPI, NAVAJO, PUEBLO, YAQUI, ZUNI

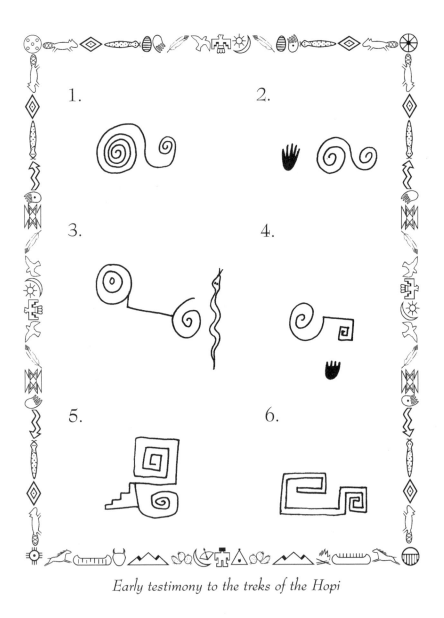

1.

2.

3.

4.

5.

6.

Early testimony to the treks of the Hopi

Symbols of the Treks (Hopi)

All over the country, symbols were carved into rocks to bear witness to the treks of the people. This chapter illustrates the symbols most frequently used. The number of circles in these engravings reveals the number of journeys a nation or tribe has already made on its trek to the four corners of the Earth.

The symbol found in Oraibi (Fig. 1) shows four complete rotations one way and three rotations in the opposite direction that have already been completed on the way back.

The drawing from Chaco Canyon (Fig. 2) shows two rounds. Since the second spiral is wound in the opposite direction, it becomes clear that this group has already started on the journey back.

The symbol in Figure 3 originates with the snake tribe and was found at Gila Bend, Arizona. It shows that the group was on its third round at that point. The straight line connecting the two spirals reveals that the group remained at this place for some time.

The engraving left by the badger tribe (Fig. 4) has a similar meaning and contains the additional information that the group had come from the South. It was found in Mesa Verde, Colorado.

The symbol at Springerville, Arizona (Fig. 5) represents three complete rounds. The stair motif indicates the construction of a village. The symbol also tells of the return of the tribe to its starting point.

The symbol in Figure 6 was discovered at Chichén Itzá. It shows that the group returned to the same area from where it came after completing only one round. This drawing reinforces the Hopi belief that the Maya were in fact disloyal Hopi who did not complete their treks.

45

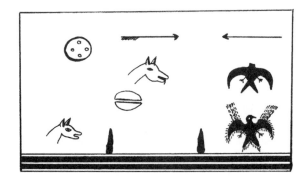

Symbols of treks and competitions

Symbols of the Coyote Clan of the Hopi

The top picture was found in a ruined *kiva* (p. 59). The five horizontal lines forming the bottom border are colored black to represent the underworld. Blue represents water, red represents the
Earth, yellow represent fertile topsoil, and white represents the Sun.
Two black obsidian knives are on top of these lines. Next to the left
knife is the head of a coyote. Next to the right knife is a swallow
with rain falling down on it. Above it is a beheaded swallow.
Opposite of the beheaded swallow is the head of a coyote again. The
oval object below the coyote, which is split in two, represents the
taweyah—the magic shield that allowed people to travel through the
air. On the top left-hand corner is a circle with four dots, which represents the four leaders of the Coyote Clan and praying for their
success. Two arrows border the top of the painting. The picture as
a whole describes a race between the Coyote and Swallow Clans.

The various representations of a coyote in the second picture are
symbols of the clan's treks. The coyote from Oraibi (Fig. 1) shows
that the clan has completed all four rounds and found a place for a
permanent settlement. This is symbolized by the coyote's tail pointing to the center of the circle. The picture from Chaco Canyon (Fig.
2) indicates that the clan at that time had only completed the second
round in its journey (two circles). In front of the coyote from the
Ventana cave in Arizona (Fig. 3), we can see the four-pronged star
of haste, warning people that they must complete the four rounds of
their journey quickly. The two coyotes from Gila Bend (Fig. 4) tell
of the tribe traveling first in one direction and then returning. The
coyote from Springerville (Fig. 5) indicates with its stuck-out tongue
that this clan had hurried ahead of the others to find a place of settlement. This was one of the duties of the Coyote Clan.

47

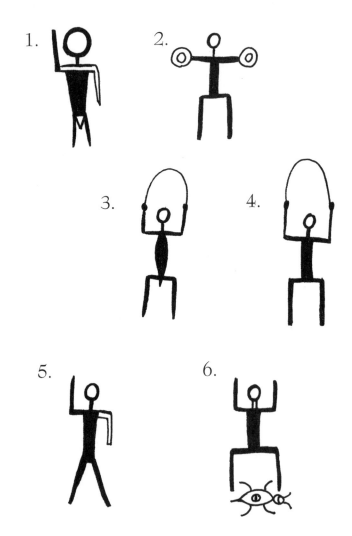

Symbols of human leaders

The Religious Leaders of the Hopi

The pictures of a man, which were found in almost every ruin of the Hopi culture, generally represent the religious leader of the respective village's main tribe.

As a sign that they were men who acted responsibly, Figures 1 and 5 are drawn with their right arms lifted. This means that they were able to perform the ceremonies with such accuracy and diligence that there was always plenty of rainfall, which resulted in good harvests. Figure 1 was found near Oraibi, Figure 5 near Gila Bend.

The leader from Chaco Canyon (Fig. 2) bears the additional feature of two circles at the ends of his extended arms. This indicates that he and his people have only completed two rounds on their trek.

Figures 3 and 4 from Texas and Mesa Verde, respectively, are shown with the addition of a curved line above their heads. This curved line is called *equilni* and represents the strap with which the leader carried valuables and ritual items on his back. This in turn refers to the great responsibility the leader quite literally had to shoulder.

The spider symbol shown below the drawing of a man from Springerville (Fig. 6) identifies him as the leader of the spider tribe.

Symbol of cosmic harmony

The Hopi Kachina Rattle

The round, flat front of the gourd rattle represents the Earth, whereas the circle on the inside stands for the Sun and its life-giving rays. If the swastika rotates to the left, as can be seen on the illustration, it represents the Sun. If it rotates to the right, it stands for the Earth.

The North-South axis of the Earth is symbolized by the staff that goes through the gourd and serves as a handle. At the ends of the Earth's axis live the two heroic twins *Pöqánghoya* and *Palöngawhoya*, who constantly emit harmony-creating vibrations along the axis and, therefore, cause the Earth to continue moving. The star constellations of the Milky Way are represented by the markings on the outer rim of the rattle.

The rattling sound is used as a signal by the *kachinas* (p. 53), for example, as a warning or for an announcement. After their initiation to the *kachina* or *powamu* bands, children are given simple rattles similar to those of the *kachinas*.

51

I.
*Divine Hopi messengers (*kachinas)

Traditional Hopi Kachina Masks (1)

Kachinas are the spirits of the invisible life forces. They are supernatural beings who mediate between the gods and the people who live on Earth. As divine messengers, they live among the people between the winter and summer solstice where their task is to create order. During this time, they are the focus of ceremonies and rituals. They relay the wishes of the people to the gods—be it for more rain, a plentiful harvest, or being spared from diseases. After the sowing and ripening season, the *kachinas* return to their homes high above the San Francisco mountains.

As soon as a Hopi has donned the mask and clothes of a *kachina*, he is regarded, according to the deeply-rooted beliefs of his tribe, as a perfect divine messenger whose human characteristics have been transformed into the ancestral spirit of a *kachina*. The male inhabitants of a village who take on the personas of the *kachinas* embody both good and evil, encouraging people to imitate the good and warning them to refrain from the evil. They are generally regarded as benevolent beings, but are both respected and feared by the Hopi and, as such, also play an important part in the children's upbringing. Sometimes they amuse the people by acting out crude jokes with a serious connotation, and they have the power to punish any wrongdoing. *Kachinas* appear wearing masks of animals, plants, stars, demons, warriors, clowns, or mythical beings.

Examples of *kachina* masks on the opposite page:
1. Three-horned *kachina*   2. Scorpio *kachina*
3. Mountain sheep *kachina*   4. Broad-faced *kachina*
5. Black mask   6. Heheya *kachina* girl
7. Snow *kachina*   8. Early morning *kachina*

II.
Divine Hopi messengers (kachinas)

Traditional Hopi Kachina Masks (2)

Kachina masks are made of wood, leather, or cotton. They are decorated with appliqué or painted ornaments, which serve to distinguish individual symbolic figures clearly.

The presentation of the traditional costume is prescribed by tradition just as much as that of the masks. Usually, knee-length white cotton skirts are worn with the masks, and they are decorated with woven strips featuring the traditional Hopi colors of black, green, and red. In addition, a cloak or a fox skin is worn around the shoulders.

Additional outfitting consists of rattles made of dried gourds, miniature bows and arrows, prayer sticks, tortoise shields, and an evergreen sprig as a symbol of the fertile and wooded homeland whence the ancestors came a long time ago.

Other important accessories are pieces of silver jewelry set with turquoise in the shape of bracelets, necklaces, or belts. These are worn for adornment.

The significance of the *kachina* masks shown on the opposite page:

1. Saviki
2. Soyoko
3. Seed-god *kachina*
4. Tasaf Anya
5. Flute *kachina*
6. Hano clown
7. *Kachina* mother
8. Sun *kachina*

Common symbols of ascent and rebirth

Mother Earth Symbols of the Hopi

The opposite page shows symbols of ascent. Both drawings are generally known as *Tápuat*, mother and child. The square shape represents the spiritual rebirth from one world to the next. In this depiction, the straight line that emerges from the entrance is not connected to the labyrinth. The two ends of this line stand for the two stages in life: the unborn child in the mother's womb and the child after it has been born. The line itself represents the umbilical cord and the path of moving upwards. The bottom end of the line is surrounded by a U shape, which is part of the labyrinth and which represents the amniotic sack that surrounds the embryo. The outer lines symbolize the arms of the mother holding her child.

In the circular shape, the central line at the entrance is connected directly to the labyrinth. The resulting cross in the center is symbolic of the Father Sun, the giver of life. In this depiction, the lines of the labyrinth come to an end in four different points. These represent the cardinal points, which are enclosed by the all-encompassing plan of the creator. The "double security" or rebirth is guaranteed for those who follow the path of the creator, and this in turn is shown here through the child surrounded by his mother's arms. Furthermore, the round shape also reveals the concentric circles of the land to which the Hopi have traditionally laid claim.

Both shapes have been passed down the generations through engravings in rock. They can also be found together on the wooden staff, which is planted in front of the unicorn altar in the *kwani kiva* during the *wúwuchim* ceremony (see p. 59). During this ceremony, the priest circles the village four times in order to take ritual possession of the ground in accordance with the all-encompassing plan.

This symbol generally carries the same meaning for all other native tribes in North, Central and South America.

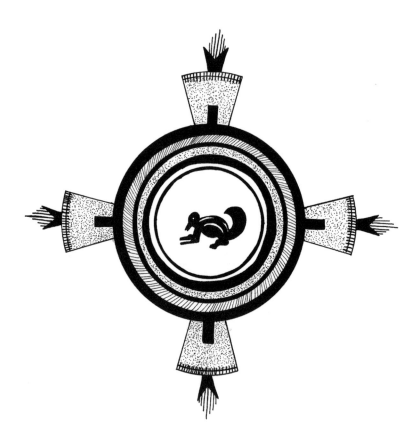

Hopi symbol of the life-giving power of the Sun

The Skunk from the Potter's Hill (Hopi)

This depiction of a skunk was found on the wall of a *kiva*, an underground ceremonial chamber. Since the Snake Band and the Two-Horn Band are the only two religious bands among the Hopi who have the skunk as a ritual symbol, it can be safely assumed that the picture originated with the Two-Horn Band of the Bow Clan.

The center of the picture has a skunk holding a *nacha*, a pair of wooden tongs, in its front paws. The *nacha* is used during the ceremony of "New Fire" to carry the glowing coals from the Two-Horn *kiva* to the three other *kivas* involved in the ceremony—the *kivas* of the Unicorn Clan, the Flute Clan, and the *Wuchim*. There, the ritual fires are lit.

The skunk itself is regarded as a representative of the Sun, as its strong smell pervades everything, like the rays of the Sun, reaching out into the whole world and giving life to all creatures. This characteristic is reinforced by the stripes on the back of the skunk, which are called Sun shields and show the face of the Sun or the creator.

The inner circle (in white) represents the pure, white heat of the Sun, whereas the middle circle (in orange, here represented by dots) stands for growth-promoting heat. The outermost circle that connects the four fire pits symbolizes the Sun itself and the four fires in the *kivas* that originate from it. Its color is a dark red.

The four fires burn at the four points of the compass in the four *kivas*. The fire pits are represented by the four small rectangles. Four eagles' feathers, which emerge from the four fire pits, reflect the power of the ceremony.

1.

2.

Hopi symbols of fertility and beauty

Symbols of the Hopi Deities Panaiyoikyasi and Kuwánlelenta

The rock painting in Figure 1 shows an insect inside a flower and asserts the benevolent aspect of *Panaiyoikyasi*'s power. *Panaiyoikyasi* means "short rainbow," and he is the deity of the Water Clan. This god holds power over the atmosphere when the Sun shines and over the Earth when the rain falls, because he is the link between sky and Earth. It is his creative power that makes plants beautiful and gives the flowers their pollen, on which in turn the life of the insects depends.

This painting also depicts *Kuwánlelenta*: "He who creates a beautiful environment." He is the guardian spirit of the sunflowers and the deity of the Sunflower Clan.

Figure 2 shows a clay vessel decorated with sunflower girls. Sunflowers are regarded as living beings that are brought to life by Father Sun and the gods.

Since the face of the flower is round, it embodies the female aspect. This is why during the Hopi women's ceremony, the *Owaqlt*, two girls, whose faces have been painted with crushed sunflower petals, enter the ceremonial square. Sunflowers are of great significance in Hopi tradition.

61

1.

2.

3.

Symbols of guardian snakes

Snake Symbolism of Different Tribes in the Southwest

The thunderstorm snake of the Tewa (Fig. 1) originated in the Southwest of the United States. Snakes are often associated with flashes of lightning and are feared both for their speed and their deadly power.

The water snake of the South (Fig. 2) is a symbol of the Snake Clan of the Hopi, who left this image on a rock near Oraibi. The lines that divide the body of the snake into several sections are equated with parts of the human body. The ritual of the Snake of the South is still carried out in the *kivas* of the first mesa, on the occasion of the *Pámuya* ceremony. The snake is called *Pálulukang*. In the past, it protected the people on their treks through the Southern region.

The snake hill (Fig. 3) is situated near Louden, Ohio. This snake embodies the guardian of the East and is called *Tokchi'i*. It is the largest depiction of a snake worldwide, and the Hopi are convinced that it was created by their ancestors. It is an earthwork about 1320 feet long, 20 feet wide, and 5 feet high. The winding body of the snake describes a wide curve. Between its open jaws, an oval hill nestles. According to the interpretation of the Snake Clan, this hill represents the village that the snake protects. The extension coming forth from the jaw indicates that the snake has the power to attract light. The two smaller hillocks on both sides of the head represent the snake's eyes. The snake faces westward in order to protect the people on their trek until they have reached the mountains that separate the East from the West.

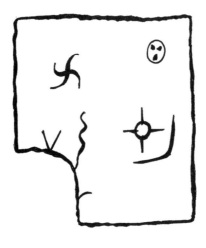

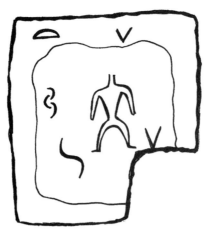

Hopi clan slate with prophetic significance

The Holy Slate of the Fire Clan

After the ascension of the people into the fourth world, their guardian spirit *Másaw* instructed them on how to conduct their treks and how to find their future home. This was inscribed on holy slates.

The Fire Clan of the Hopi received from its guardian spirit a very small slate about 4 inches long, from which one corner had been broken. On this slate, a number of symbols and a body without a head were drawn. The symbols predict that the Fire Clan will one day, after it has reached its final destination, be conquered by strange people. The people of the Fire Clan will then be forced to live according to the laws of the new rulers. They should not try to resist, however, but wait for the person who will free them. This referred to the lost white brother *Pahána*. He would return with the missing piece from the slate and, together with the Fire Clan, would find a worldwide brotherhood of men. If, however, the leader of the Fire Clan had accepted a new, foreign religion, he would have to agree to be beheaded so that evil could be driven away and his people would be saved.

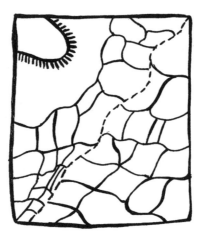

Holy slate of the Hopi

The First Slate of the Bear Clan

The Bear Clan was meant to be the leading Hopi clan in the fourth world. For this reason, its god, *Söqömhonaw*, gave them three prophetic slates before he became invisible once again.

The first slate, the smallest of them all, shows an irregular pattern on the front, representing the fields surrounding the future home village. This was to be the way in which the land would be distributed among the various clans after the Bear Clan completed its treks.

On the other side is a picture of two bear's paws, indicating that any land outside the boundaries shown on the front of the slate should be managed by the Bear Clan. This was to ensure the preservation of the animal kingdom, as the lives of the people also depended on its survival.

Holy slate of the Hopi referring to their future home

The Second Slate of the Bear Clan

This larger slate of the Bear Clan shows two snakes on the front encircling land where corn grows and various animals live. The snakes represent two rivers, which will be the boundaries of the future home of the Bear Clan.

In the four corners of the slate are the pictures of four men, each extending an arm and pointing to the land. These are the four religious leaders who will lay claim to the land on behalf of their people. Furthermore, nobody will be allowed to cross the boundaries of the land without their permission; otherwise, great misfortune would threaten all those who live on the land.

The back of the slate indicates that the leader of the village should always be of the Bear Clan.

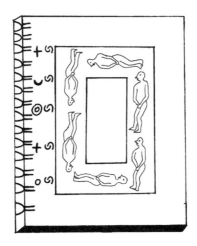

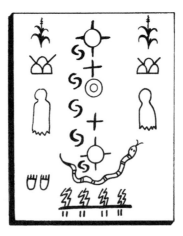

Spiritual slate of the Hopi

The Third Holy Slate of the Bear Clan

The six men arranged inside the rectangle represent the leaders of the most important Hopi clans. The side of the slate is carved with notches and also shows the symbols of Sun, Moon, Earth and stars. To the right of these, the *nakwách* symbol can be seen. This is meant to point to a brotherly union, in this case, with the universe. The two rectangles again represent the two rivers that form the boundaries of the village.

The back of the slate has been decorated with a multitude of symbols, the meaning of which is not entirely clear. In the middle, a number of cosmic motifs can be found, which link to the *nakwách* symbol of brotherhood. Above these symbols to the left and right there are cornstalks and, below them, rain clouds to ensure the survival of humans, animals, and plants. The figures below the rain clouds are probably a representation of spiritual beings. The snake and zigzag lines stand for rivers and rainwater. To the left of them, the footprints of a bear stand for the great responsibility that the Bear Clan carries within the cosmic fabric.

In summary, it can be assumed that this slate serves as an indication as to how man can achieve and maintain a life in harmony with the universe.

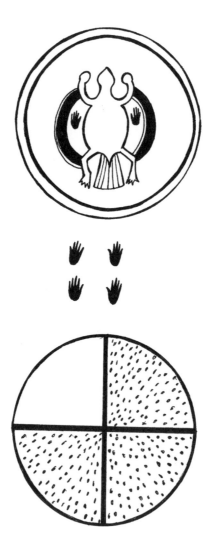

Representation of the rain god

Rock Drawing by the Fire Clan of the Hopi

This rock drawing was found in the village of Betatakin, which the Fire Clan built a long time ago, inside a huge cave. Among others, the image of *Taknokwumu*, the spirit that rules the weather, was discovered. His arms and legs are connected by rainbow stripes, and the whole figure is arranged inside a shield.

The second drawing gives us the reason for this representation of *Taknokwumu*. Three quarters of the circle, which represents the land in the area, are painted red. This points to the fact that this area was completely dried out at that time, due to lack of rain. And indeed, these cave paintings were created during the great drought approximately between 1242 and 1300.

The four handprints show that the Fire Clan had, at that time, completed the fourth round of its journey and was on its way to Oraibi.

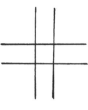

Kiva paintings supply a background for ceremonies

Hopi Corn Mural

The layout of this mural is known as a ritual house. Today, the Hopi rarely use murals; they have largely been substituted by sand pictures, which carry the same meaning and are created afresh for every ceremony under the altar of the main *kiva*.

The mural on the opposite page was discovered in Awatovi and was used during the *soyál* ceremony in which the corn was blessed. The eleven clans who took part in this ceremony in Awatovi are represented by eleven cobs of corn. Below the cobs of corn is a brown-colored stripe that represents the warm Earth. The black stripe below represents the depth to which the water filters through to ensure the growth of the corn. The two pictures in the corners show the sticks used by those who performed the ritual.

During the time of the *soyál* ceremony, corn was gathered in every house and, after being blessed by the chief, piled up below the altar of the main *kiva*.

The cobs of corn in this picture are painted in the colors attributed to the directions of the wind-white, red, blue, and yellow. The hatching between the brown and the black stripe represents the corn-mother, the most perfect cob of corn. The cross symbol below the picture represents life in perfection.

Kiva mural of the Hopi, illustrating the significance of the Eagle Clan

Mural of the Eagle Clan

The two spheres, which the eagle clutches in its claws, embody the present and future worlds. Both worlds are immersed in the power of water, which is represented by the broad, hatched stripe painted below it. Below the figure of the eagle is a stylized representation of a skunk. On the left is the symbol of the Sun, which, to this day, is painted just like this onto *kachina* rattles. On the right is the symbol of the Earth, divided into four colored segments, representing the four directions of the wind.

The item to the right of the eagle represents a jug with corn seeds. On top of it lies a squash, also full of seeds.

Since this mural was also discovered in a *kiva* in the village of Awatovi, it becomes clear that the Eagle Clan played an important role there as well.

(In the original painting, the head of the eagle was missing from being destroyed by weather. In the drawing on the opposite page, it has been replaced by a replica.)

The Hopi swallow ritual

Mural with Swallows

During the *wúwuchim* ceremony, the Hawk Clan used swallow feathers to send messages to the gods, because swallows were regarded as the fastest birds in the world.

The swallow on the far left rises up to the sky along a black line that marks its path. The black line crossing its path indicates that this is happening before nightfall. The seven dots right next to the bird's beak represent the Pleiades, while the cluster of nine dots situated between the two birds stands for the nine stars of the Northern Crown, the *lakón*. This name has also been adopted by one of the women's bands.

The second swallow indicates that the ceremony has lasted beyond midnight. On the one hand, the line crossing its path is much longer; on the other hand, the nine stars of the lakón can now be found right next to the swallow's head. The Pleiades have already disappeared from view altogether.

The rituals in the Hopi *kivas* always depended on the position of the stars in the sky.

1.

2.

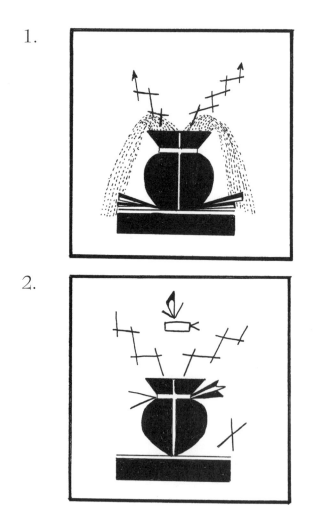

The Hopi's magical water jug, which provides the people with water wherever they are.

The Ritual Water Jug

Figure 1 shows the ritual water jug used by women. It is recognized by its rounded base. The water in this picture is represented by broken lines.

The water jug of the male leader (Fig. 2) has a pointed base so that it can be pushed into the ground more easily. In this picture, the water is represented by splashes on the left of the magic jug.

In ancient times, before the Hopi even started their treks, the magic water jug, or the *móngwikoro*, was given to each clan by the god of the Fire Clan. *Másaw* instructed the people to choose a holy person in each clan who would assume responsibility for the divine water jug. This holy person would have to pray and live without salt for 4 days before the clan moved on and another 4 days once the clan arrived at its destination. After that, the water bearer would be able to place the jug in the ground, and the water would flow once again.

In case the jug was lost or destroyed, *Másaw* also gave the clan very specific ritual instructions on how to make a new jug. During the ceremony, various parts of the sea needed to be added to the jug. This would ensure that even in a desert, the people would have a never-ending supply of water, which the jug would attract, from the sea.

Másaw said that, in later years, many people would wonder why the Hopi often built villages in areas known for their aridness. But these people knew nothing about the sacred jug or the prayers.

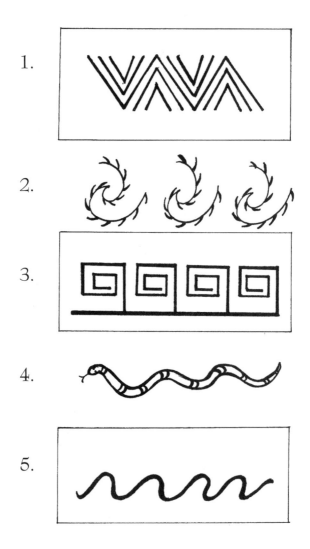

1.

2.

3.

4.

5.

Depictions of water shared by different tribes

Symbols of Water

All the symbols on the opposite page can be found in Hopi rock paintings, but they were also used by other tribes.

Figure 1 shows calm water, Figure 3 represents big waves, and Figure 5 describes rough water.

Figure 2 shows marks left by the Water Clan of the Hopi. It shows whirls in the water. The number of whirls indicates how many rounds the clan has already traveled on its journey. This engraving is part of a very old rock picture.

Snake motifs, such as in Figure 4, are often used to mark rivers. However, the Water Clan of the Hopi also claims this symbol for itself.

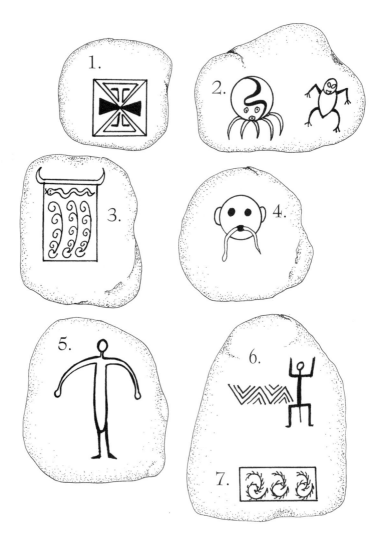

Different clan symbols within the Hopi tribe

Hopi Rock Drawings

Figure 1 shows the symbol of the Butterfly Clan, representing a stylized butterfly. Figure 2 shows rock pictures of the Spider Clan. On the left is a representation of a spider; on the right is a picture of its offspring, which has just hatched.

The symbol in Figure 3 indicates the presence of the Snake Clan. The stylized plants below the snake stand for an abundant supply of food.

Figure 4 shows the deity of the Bow Clan bearing a snake in his mouth. This deity is *Sáviki*, a belligerent being who had an evil face and wore dark clothes. After he had instigated an attack on the Snake and Lizard Clans but lost, these two clans stripped him of his symbol, the bow, and put instead a snake in his mouth. Since then, *Sáviki* has been represented in this fashion.

Figure 5 shows the deity of the Fire Clan. With his outstretched arms, he indicates that the Fire Clan has driven away the Water Clan from its territory and has blocked the way back.

Figures 6 and 7 are markings by the Water Clan. Figure 6 shows the emblem of the Water Clan: the zigzag lines on the left symbolize water and the figure on the right bearing a tail represents a tadpole just before it casts off its tail to become a frog.

The three water whirls in Figure 7 tell of the fact that the Water Clan has already reached the sea shores three times and at the time was on the third round of its trek.

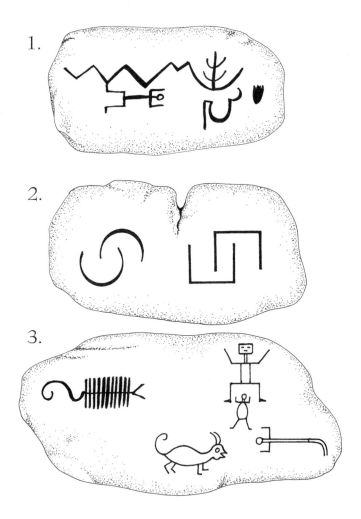

Representations of important events and the symbols of brotherhood

Rock Pictures of Various Hopi Clans

Figure 1 tells the story of the death of *Salavi*, who was the old leader of the Badger Clan. To indicate his passing, the picture shows him in a horizontal position. The zigzag line above him symbolizes the life-giving water, out of which a fir tree grows. It is believed that the dying *Salavi* was transformed into this fir tree. Since the fir is revered as a holy tree, possessing the greatest magnetic power, it is always shown with an upright trunk and branches that point upwards. Below the fir tree, *Salavi*'s life line can be seen rising from Mother Earth after his birth to be absorbed as a spirit into the roots of the tree. The footprint on the right indicates the migration of *Salavi*'s people.

Figure 2 shows two versions of the *nakwách* symbol, which is a symbol of brotherhood. To this day, during the *wúwuchim* ceremony, priests form this symbol during their dance.

Figure 3 was carved into rock by the Deep Well Clan and tells of their leaving the village of Wenima. The symbol on the left represents the treks of the people and their stay in Wenima, which lasted several years. The vertical lines stand for the number of years spent in Wenima. The fork at the right hand end of the symbol indicates that the clan split up when the people moved on. On the right hand side of the picture, there is a likeness of the god *Panaiyoikyasi* suspended above the image of a man as he accompanied the clan on its journey. In addition, the god is represented in the bottom right hand corner, this time, in a horizontal position, which means he can continue to protect the deserted village spiritually.

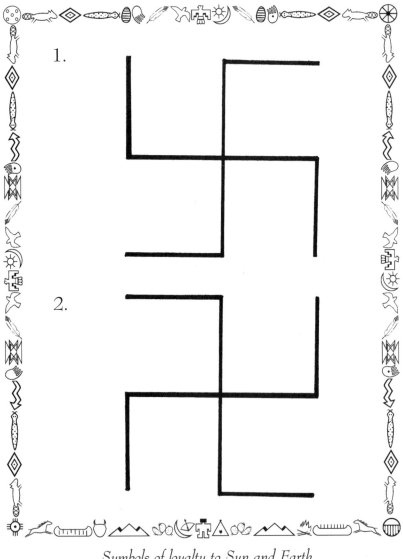

1.

2.

Symbols of loyalty to Sun and Earth

Migration Patterns of the Hopi Clans

All Hopi clans started their treks in Túwanasavi. This place is not at the geographical center of North America; rather, it should be understood as a mental and spiritual center. This is why Túwanasavi is regarded as the center of the world. It is here that, according to the legends, the migrations of the individual clans started along the North-South axle and along the East-West axle. The treks, therefore, describe the shape of a large cross, ending with the arctic in the North, the Pacific coast in the West, the Atlantic coast in the East, and the Gulf of Mexico in the South. When the leading clans reached these end points, they turned right and only then started their way back. Consequently, the large cross became a large swastika, which turns to the left like a water wheel and, therefore, represents the Earth (Fig. 1).

Since the leading clans held more knowledge and were the first to start the migrations, they laid claim to the land. Of all the clans, only seven reached the southern tip of South America: the Bear, Eagle, Sun, Kachina, Parrot, Flute, and Coyote Clans. Among the other leading clans were the Snake, Spider, Tobacco, Water, and Bow Clans.

The less important clans turned left at the end of their treks. They simply greeted the Sun in their prayers and supported the leading clans in their ceremonies, since they did not have any complete rituals themselves. By turning left, the path of these clans formed a swastika that turns clockwise—that is, with the Sun (Fig. 2). In this fashion, the clans professed their loyalty to their creator, the Father Sun. Among these clans are: the Mole, Bluebird, Sparrow Hawk, Butterfly, Crow, Millet, Pumpkin, Shallow Well, Fog, Sun, Sand, and Corn Clans.

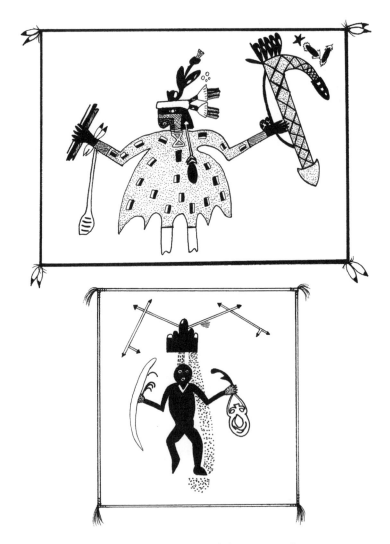

Creator and keeper of the Hopi tribe

Qaletaqa and Pöqánghoya

The top figure shows the traditional guardian of the Hopi. His name is *Qaletaqa*. The white, pleated gaiters that he wears on his lower legs indicate that he is a member of the Coyote Clan. He is also carrying a *hótango*, a quiver, and arrows. He wears clothing made of goat's skin.

Pöqánghoya, one of the two heroic twins, is shown in the bottom figure. He is always represented in dark, Earth colors, since it was he who was given the task to make the Earth become firm. He is easily recognized by the crooked staff that he carries, the *makwanpi*, with which he pointed to the Earth and said, "You shall become firm." The white shield, which he holds in his left hand, protects him from evil influences. His great power is illustrated by the flashes of lightning and the massive cloud above his head. The dotted lines symbolize the falling rain.

According to the legend, the twins *Pöqánghoya* and *Palöngawhoya* were the first living beings on the newly created Earth. They themselves were created by the "spider woman" from a little Earth and saliva. While *Pöqánghoya*, the older twin, went about his task of making the Earth become firm, his brother went out into the world, sending out sacred exclamations and sounds that echoed the praise for the creator of all things. His task was to maintain order in the world. He is also called "echo," since all sounds are the echo of the creator.

1.

2.

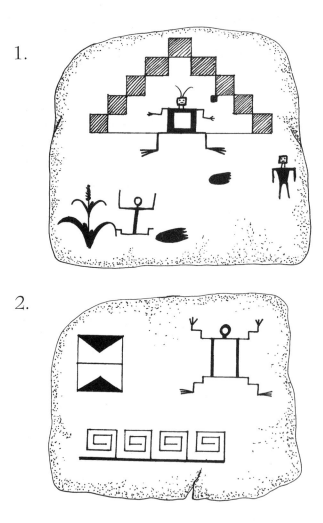

Representations of the god Panaiyoikyasi

Rock Pictures of the Deep Well Clan and the Water Clan of the Hopi

Figure 1 shows the god *Panaiyoikyasi* at the center of a triangle just as he is forming a spiritual alliance with the people. The small black square indicates that the vault where the picture of the deity is kept is at a secret location. The two smaller figures in the bottom section of the picture indicate the presence of the Shallow and the Deep Well Clans.

One of the basic foodstuffs was corn, which is represented in the bottom left-hand corner of the drawing. The horizontal footprints indicate that the clans have stayed at this location for a while (vertical footprints would have meant that the clans moved on). This rock picture was found in the old village of Wenima.

Another picture, also discovered near Wenima, again shows the god *Panaiyoikyasi* (Fig. 2). Here, he has been placed at the top right of the picture. The other two symbols in the picture indicate the presence of the Water Clan, who also revered this deity. The drawing in the top left corner represents a cloud reflected in water. This reflection is repeated in the drawing of the deity on the right with his raised arms forming the symbol of cloud terraces that is reflected in the shape of his legs.

The four large water waves below stand for the four journeys that the Water Clan had to complete.

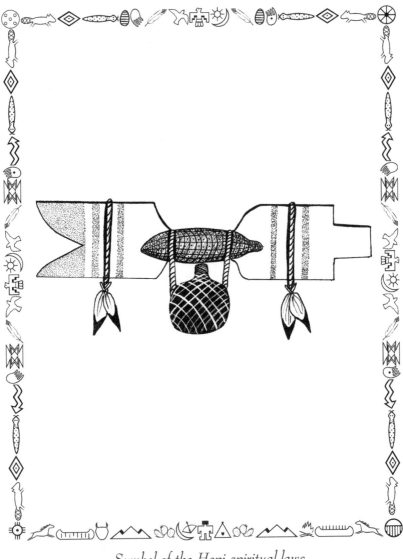

Symbol of the Hopi spiritual laws

The Two-Horn Mongko

The *mongko* is the highest symbol of spiritual power. It serves as proof to all clans and bands who own it that they have completed their century-long migration. It is the highest law of the Hopi. Only the Two-Horn, the Unicorn, and the Flute Bands own ritual *mongkos*. The Two-Horn *mongko* shown on the opposite page is made of a flat piece of wood, which has been painted white. The forked section on the left is painted blue to represent all the plants that cover the Earth. The other blue lines stand for water. On the other side, the stepped end tells of the three main guidelines in Hopi law: respect, harmony, and love. An entire cob of corn is attached to the center of the *mongko* as a symbol of man. A small sphere filled with Earth hangs from the cob of corn; it contains a small drop of water and is bound by a cotton net. This sphere represents the Earth and the sea. Furthermore, there are four turkey feathers tied to the wood, pointing to the fact that the wild turkey is part of the wilderness of this Earth, and that man will never quite understand this wilderness nor will he ever completely rule it.

The smallest *mongko* is only 4 inches long. A medium size one is about 16 inches long and is carried by every member of the band during the rituals. The largest *mongko* is over 3 feet long and is used exclusively to block the entrance to the *kivas* while initiation rites are occurring inside.

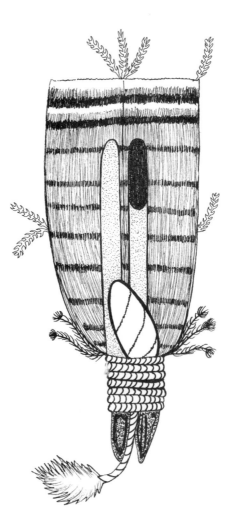

Prayer feather of the Hopi

Male-female Páho

The *páho* embodies the invisible vibrations of prayer. Until this energy is absorbed by the life powers, the *páho* is kept in a sacred place or is hidden in a rock crevice or bush. Every *páho* only serves ritual purposes alone. Prayers accompany its making.

The figure on the opposite page shows a male-female *páho*, which is made up of two small red willow sticks that were dyed blue. The female stick has a flattened end, which has been painted brown. Both sticks are tied at the lower end to a small pouch made of corn-husks. This pouch represents the spiritual body. It contains corn meal as a symbol of the physical body, pollen of the corn plant as a symbol of fertility, and a drop of honey to symbolize the love of the creator. Both sticks are tied together with cotton string to represent the thread of life. In this manner, male and female powers are united. At the end of the string, an eagle's down feather is attached, which stands for the breath of life. A long string tells of a long life.

The bright blue color stands for the spiritual characteristics of the sky, water, and plant life. The dye is produced from the colored Earth in a salt cave of the Grand Canyon. The brown dye, the color of Mother Earth, is taken from the Grand Canyon as well. The lower part of the *páho* is painted with black dye, which is obtained from weathered stone. This lower part of the *páho* is "planted" into the Earth to symbolize that man is rooted in this world as long as he is in it.

In addition, a turkey feather is fastened to the *páho* to reflect the wildness and secrets of creation. The small twigs, the *chamisa* and the *kúnya*, represent the heat of the summer and the healing of illnesses.

1.

2.

3.

Representations of the wúwuchim ceremony of the Hopi

Cave Paintings of the Unicorn and Two-Horn Bands

All the representations on the opposite page refer to the night of the hair-washing ceremony during the *wúwuchim* ceremony. During that night, members of the Two-Horn Band used to patrol the village around the guarded *kiva* in group of two, accompanied by their godfathers.

Figure 1 shows a painting by the Two-Horn Band from Mesa Verde; the drawings in Figure 2 are taken from a rock picture on the steep banks of the Colorado River in Utah. Both pictures represent two people about to be initiated, accompanied by their godfather. His task is to protect them from negative influences. He is represented in each picture as the smaller figure on the right.

The person in the center of Figure 2 carries an oval item to represent the water jug of the chief, which, during the course of the ceremony, is emptied into a small hole in the ground.

Figure 3 was found in a cave in El Paso County, Texas. The two figures on the left are recognizable as members of the Unicorn Band. Both have been painted with red mineral paint. To their right is a member of the Two-Horn Band.

The ceremonies, which are carried out to this day by members of the Unicorn and the Two-Horn Bands as well as the Bow Clan, are among the most significant ceremonies of each year.

Divine Hopi messenger

The Hopi God of the Arrow Shaft Clan

This mural on the opposite page tells the story of how the highest deity of the Arrow Shaft Clan presented the *páhos* to the highest being, which had previously been used in the very complex ritual of the *wúwuchim*. The feathers were taken from the wings of a sparrow hawk, embodying the bird's strength and speed.

Since this spiritual being travels through dimensions that are inconceivable to the human mind, it is shown with black skin to indicate that some kind of divine messenger is represented. His connection to the people of the Arrow Shaft Clan and the Bow Clan in Oraibi and Awatovi is made clear through the symbols of two lightning flashes hanging from his side. He is holding in his hand the two *páhos* that he has just received.

1.

2.

Spiritual paintings of the Zuni refer to the
life beyond of the deceased

Painted Zuni Clay Pots

The painting in Figure 1 shows a feathered cloud. This stands for a prayer asking a deceased person to assume the shape of a cloud and return with rain and thunder.

According to Zuni beliefs, the *kachinas*, who possessed their own masks while they were alive, are able to return to their spiritual form by inhabiting the mask of a dancer who is still alive. All other inhabitants of a *kachina* village can return in the shape of a rain cloud. If the inhabitants of a *kachina* village are not currently traveling to Zuni as rain clouds, they lead a normal life that is very similar to the life of the person that they once were. Nevertheless, they are closer to the "raw" world than the living are. This is first expressed in a loss of their unmistakable identity, as they no longer have a personality but only represent a certain type of person without individual faces. A person who dies and moves on to the *kachina* village will never be called by his own name again. Also, most of those who live in the *kachina* village are no longer able to speak. Instead, they use animal sounds, such as the bellow of the stag.

In Figure 2, a stag is drawn according to Zuni tradition with its heart line shown. Members of the *kachina* society had the opportunity to be reborn as a stag and, thus, was saved from being reincarnated into lowly beings of the raw world.

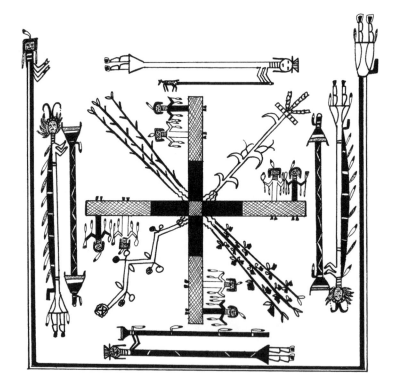

*A healing picture of the Navajo reestablishing inner
and outer harmony (hózhó)*

The World

This Navajo sandpainting is designed to help a person who is mentally or physically ill to rediscover inner and outer harmony (*hózhó*). The cross at the center represents the world with its four corners and the four elements. Furthermore, it indicates the male and the female principle: the horizontal line symbolizes the female energy, the vertical line stands for the male energy. The figures shown standing on the arms of the cross represent the world of humans. Diagonally, the four sacred nourishing plants of the Navajo are represented: corn, beans, pumpkins, and tobacco. At the four ends of the cross are the respective deities who protect the world at all sides. The picture is framed by a drawing of the rainbow spirit. This frame is open to the east in order to grant access to the positive spirits (*diyin dine'é*, meaning "holy people").

An accompanying healing chant of the Navajo refers to the extremely fragile balance between humans and spirits. It is about finding a state of harmony with the world ahead, the world behind, the world above, and the world below. A disruption of this balance may have been caused by the person himself, by other people, or by spirits.

A sand picture is created for almost every night of a ceremony, which can last up to 9 days. It's drawn in the *hogan*, the round or octagonal dwelling of the Navajo, and wiped away in the morning by the hands of the singer (*hataalii*, medicine man). The sand is swept onto a blanket, which is emptied behind the *hogan* on its North side for the wind to blow the sand away. Before that, those who attend the ceremony can each take a handful away. The sand has a healing effect and is carried in a little bag or box.

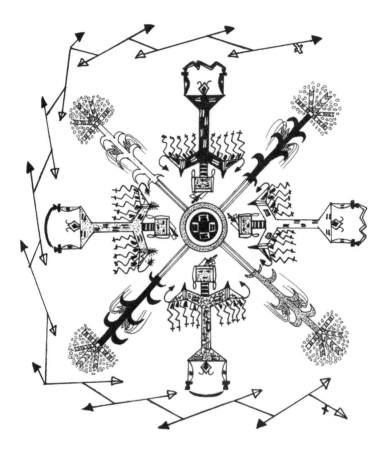

Healing picture of the Navajo designed to convey strength and power

The House of the Thunder Beings

The four thunder spirits are responsible for life-giving rain, which is caused by thunder and lightning.

This Navajo sandpainting is used during the ceremony of the shooting chant. It is a picture brimming with energy and designed to convey strength and power, including the power of asserting oneself.

The four thunder spirits, who in turn are assigned to the four cardinal points, are regarded as powerful and dangerous beings and treated with due respect. As a sign of their great power, they are shown with lightning flashing from their feet and wings, and numerous stripes, representing the rainbow, painted on their bodies.

Between the thunder spirits are the four sacred plants of the Navajo: corn, beans, pumpkin, and tobacco. The rain that is caused to fall by these thunder beings enables these plants to grow. The picture is framed and protected by stylized flashes of lightning.

The thunder spirits should not be confused with the thunderbirds of other Native American tribes. These beings are unique to Navajo mythology.

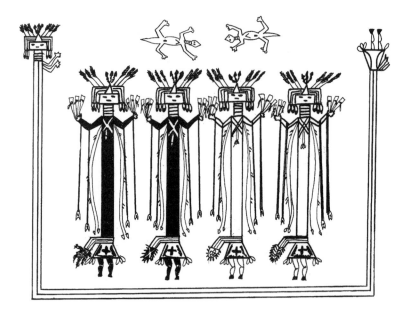

Healing picture designed to restore inner and outer harmony

The Beauty Way

This Navajo sandpainting is ruled by the sacred number Four. The four female figures that are depicted represent the four cardinal points and the four elements. It is interesting to note that in depictions by the Navajo tribe, female persons or beings are always represented with an angular head, whereas male persons or beings always have a round head. All other Native American tribes depict men and women exactly the other way round.

The two dark figures embody that side of the Earth that is in the dark, whereas the two light figures stand for that side of the Earth on which sunlight falls. The representation of dark and light refers to man's ability for good and evil. Only when these opposing powers are kept in a balance will harmony be achieved.

This healing painting is designed to restore harmony between a sick human being and the powers that surround him. During the ceremony, spiritual beings are called upon. The person concerned can identify with them and, thus, is able to overcome the disturbance. The patient will regain beauty, order, and harmony (hózhó).

The painting is framed by the spirit of the rainbow. On the East side, the entrance gateway is guarded by two water creatures.

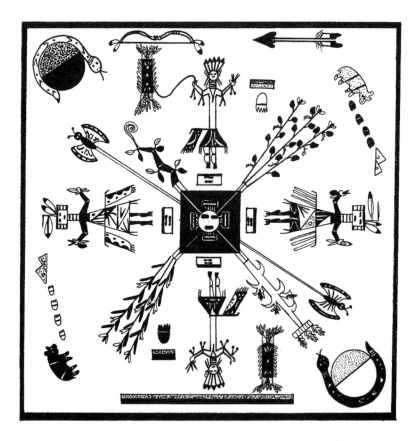

Healing painting of the Navajo

The House of the Bear and Snake

The center of this painting shows a square in which the Sun lives with the rainbow. Emerging diagonally from this square are the four sacred plants that are nourished by the Sun and the rainbow. The two figures with the angular heads represent two young women, whose beauty is emphasized by the two butterflies next to them. The *yei* (see p. 123) "Talking God," *haashch'éélti'í*, is represented by the two round-headed figures.

The snake lives in a round hut, as can be seen in the top left and bottom right hand corners of the picture. The bear, on the other hand, lives in the mountains.

The myth, upon which this sandpainting is founded, tells the story of the great snake and the bear. Once upon a time, they dressed up as old men, because they wanted to take part in an archery competition, which had two beautiful young women as the main prize. They won the contest, but could not gain the favor of the two women. Therefore, they employed a trick to seduce them: They assumed the shape of two handsome young men and, in addition, cast a love-spell over the women. However, when they turned back into old men the next morning, the two women fled. The bear and snake followed them.

This picture is used for the Blessing Way (*hózhóó'ji*), but partially also for the Beauty Way and the Mountain Way.

Universal symbol of male and female energies working together (similar to the Asian yin and yang)

Father Sky and Mother Earth

Father Sky (*yash-diklith beh-hasteen*) and Mother Earth (*nahas-tsan beh-assun*) are often featured in Navajo sandpaintings, because theirs is a special energy. They play an important role in a number of Navajo ceremonies—for example, the Mountain Way, the Blessing Way, and the Shooting Way.

Mother Earth is shown on the right. In her body, traditionally painted in turquoise, are the four sacred plants: corn, beans, pumpkin, and tobacco. The body of Father Sky shows symbols of Sun, Moon, and stars. The special power of these two deities is expressed by the horns that they carry on their heads. The zigzag line in the body of the man indicates a connection with the Milky Way.

The linking of their arms emphasizes the close relationship of the two deities. Their heads are linked by a yellow line of pollen. Also, each of them wears the color of the other in the lower half of the body: the woman wears the man's dark blue in addition to her turquoise, and vice versa.

A rainbow frames the picture to protect it, but it is open to the East so that the spirits that this picture calls upon can enter. The symbols designed to protect the open side are the medicine pouch (top left) and the bat (top right).

In Navajo paintings, the fourth side, the East side, is always shown at the top, and it is guarded by mythical creatures, guardian spirits, or guardian items.

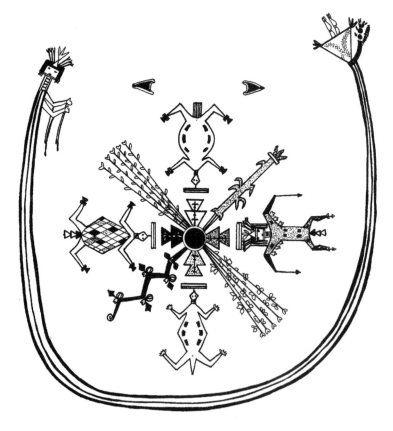

Healing picture of the Navajo for physical injury suffered from lightning or water

Water Creatures

This picture calls upon all beings that are connected with water in some way. It acknowledges the destructive power of water—for example, in sudden cloudbursts, floods, or similar—but also sees its life-giving power. Without water, plants, animals, or human beings would cease to exist. Where the Navajo live, both these aspects of water are experienced very intensively.

The myth, upon which this Navajo sandpainting (*iikááh*) is founded, tells the story of a girl, the "Younger Sister," who once went to see all the water creatures represented in this picture (see p. 127). In the upper part of the picture is the "White Water Monster." It has the shape of a whale and, according to ancient Navajo legends, lives in the ground where it controls the water supplies by creating springs, wells, and creeks.

The figure on the right represents "Blue Thunder," from which the good, nourishing rain emanates. Below is the "Great Otter," (yellow) who lives in the rivers. On the left is the "Cloud Monster," with its colorful markings. It is responsible for destructive cloudbursts.

At 45° to the deities are the four sacred plants of the Navajo: corn, beans, pumpkin, and tobacco (clockwise). The circle at the center should be interpreted as a well that is surrounded by cloud symbols (staggered triangles) on which dragonflies have settled.

The picture is protected by the rainbow being. Two stylized medicine pouches guard the open side, which faces East.

The symbolism of this painting is used to heal people who have suffered physical injury through lightning or water.

1.

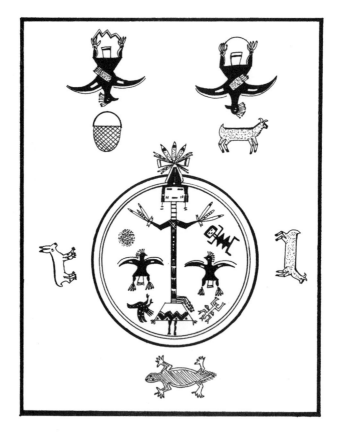

Healing sand picture accompanying the Navajo Pearl Chant

The Man in the Birds' Nest

In a myth of creation, a man went hunting with a coyote. This man had a wife and two sons. The coyote went out on his own one morning and spied an eagle's nest on a steep slope. He returned to the campsite and asked the man to help him get up to the young eagles, as he needed their feathers for his arrows. The man agreed, so the coyote let him down into the eagle's nest with the help of a rope. Once he reached the nest, however, the coyote dropped the rope and said, "Cousin, she who was your wife will now be my wife!" The man, who was in the nest with the young eagles, asked them what the weather would be like when their father returned home. They answered, "Manful rain," which means rain accompanied by thunder. Soon the father appeared accompanied by thunder and rain. After the man had explained to him his story and that he was prepared to protect the young eagles, the father eagle allowed him to stay. He brought him a vessel made of turquoise so that he could drink water. Later, the eagle mother arrived, accompanied by "female rain," meaning without thunder. She brought the man a bowl of boiled corn that replenished itself again and again.

When the eagle family gathered 4 days later, they gave the man an eagle shirt. He asked where he would go and started to sing:
Where the black reflection stands at the center of the sky, I will go up.
I will reach the shadow of the dark wings.
Where the blue reflection stands at the center of the sky, I will go up.
I will come into the shadow of the blue wings.
I will go up into the center of the sky.
I will come into the shadow of the yellow wings.
Where the white reflection stands at the center of the sky, I will go up.
I will come into the shadow of the white wings.
Between the two who sit in the white sky, I will go up.
Where the white clouds rise up white at the center of the sky, I will go up.

117

Healing sand pictures accompanying the Navajo Pearl Chant

Where the black house of the eagle stands out, that is where I come from.
Where the blue house of the eagle stands out, I will go up.
Where the yellow house of the eagle stands out, I will go up.
Where the white house of the eagle stands out, I will go up.

When they reached the realm of the sky, the eagles invited the man into one of their houses, but he declined. Instead, he went out into the night to destroy "The-one-with-the-skull-who-kills-all." Afterwards, he proceeded to kill the bees, wasps, and hornets, whose sting had the potential to kill the eagles. Furthermore, he destroyed all poisonous weeds.

When he had accomplished all these deeds, the grateful eagles showed him how to fly back to Earth. There, he met the coyote, who was living with his wife now and was treating his children badly. After he had forced the coyote to swallow two hot stones, he decided that he did not want to live on Earth any longer. He assumed the shape of the eagle again and flew back to the sky.

This story is common among the Navajo as well as among the western Apache and the Jicarilla. The Navajo version goes on to stress that the hero taught the humans the pearl chant, which he had learned from the eagle. The three sandpaintings shown on pages 116 and 118 are part of this chant. They are designed for healing purposes, especially for someone who falls ill as a result of decorating his arrows with eagle's feathers.

Figure 1 on page 116 describes the first scene from "The Man in the Birds' Nest." It shows the hero in the nest with the young eagles surrounded by animals that represent food. At the top of the painting are the eagle parents; the male eagle has a flash of lightning between his feet, the female eagle is marked by a semi-circle.

Figure 2 on the opposite page represents the ascent of the hero to the sky accompanied by male and female eagles.

Figure 3 shows the home of the eagle in the sky.

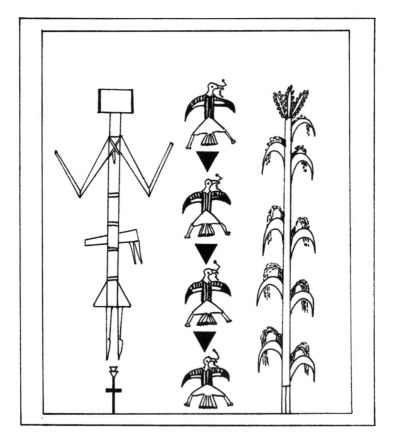

Navajo sandpainting for male rites of initiation

The Young Hero of the Navajo

This Navajo sandpainting describes a myth of ascension and is used during male initiation ceremonies. It shows a young Navajo male (on the left of the picture) who has found four eagles (middle) beyond the sky that gave him medicine. This medicine is symbolized by the black, downward-pointing triangles between the birds.

On the right of the picture is a corn plant, which stands for the food that the young Navajo received from the Hopi. Among the Native Americans of the Southwest, corn ranks highest as a food-providing plant.

The legendary bearers of culture, or the creators of the Navajo

Male and Female Yei

In Navajo mythology, the *yei* are supernatural beings who populated the Earth in the beginning and, before they left, instructed the people in many things that would make life easier for them.

The Navajo sandpainting on the opposite page shows a male *yei*, marked by a round head, and a female *yei*, marked by an angular head. Now and again, there are exceptions to this rule. The items that the *yei* carry in their hands are symbolic of life and power. The male *yei* carries lightning and a rattle, whereas the female *yei* carries a rattle and an evergreen branch, which symbolizes fertility. Both wear skirts that are adorned with pouches. Ribbons hang from their wrists and elbows.

The artist or medicine man (*hataalii* = singer) is restricted to this exact, geometric rendering when creating the painting. He can only exercise some artistic liberty when painting the pouches.

The story of the *yei* tells of how they created the first man and the first woman; they placed two cobs of corn underneath a stag skin rug, let the wind blow below it, and danced around it four times, whereupon the cobs of corn turned into human beings.

Navajo myth of creation

The Coyote Steals the Fire

The story that starts in the bottom left section of the painting forms part of the Navajo myth of creation.

The coyote steals the flame from the black god of fire, who is asleep. The white zigzag lines on the arms of the god represent the Milky Way, and below his body is the symbol of fire. The path of the coyote can be traced along the zigzag line that is connected with him.

After having stolen the fire, the coyote travels with the glowing coals through the house of the Sun, which is guarded by an eagle spirit. It then continues through the house of the Moon in the upper right hand section of the painting, and finally comes to the house of the first man and woman. The circular symbol between the two people stands for the round *hogan*, the characteristic dwelling place of the Navajo, to which the coyote carries the fire.

The coyote plays a significant role in many Native American legends. Traditionally, it is regarded as a cunning rascal who is always trying to get the better of others. Its character is very similar to Reynard the Fox in European fables. However, it can also assume the role of the hero, as in this story, and become the helper of man. These traits are personified by one and the same character in the legends of many tribes.

Protecting and healing painting of the Navajo

The Endless Snake

The snake makes its appearance in many sand- and healing paintings, because it is respected as the symbol of renewal and rebirth, embracing both life and death.

Furthermore, it is linked with healing and with the knowledge of secret matters, as well as with fertility and rain.

On the sandpainting on the opposite page, the endless snake is located in the center and is decorated with splashes of the sacred colors white, blue, yellow, red, and black. Its Navajo name is *klish-do-nuti'i*. It is protected by the guardian snakes of the four cardinal points. The white snake stands for the dawn and, therefore, for the East; the yellow snake stands for the dusk and, therefore, for the West. The black snake embodies darkness and, therefore, the North; whereas the blue snake embodies the sky and, therefore, the South.

The painting is open to the East and is guarded against intruders by a black water jug and a white cloud. The guardian spirit of the Black Snake encloses the painting and, like the Endless Snake in the middle, it is decorated with the sacred colors.

The myth, upon which this painting is founded, tells the story of a girl, the "Younger Sister" (see p. 115) who spent a night in a cave with snakes.

4

The Plains

ARAPAHO, CHEYENNE, COMANCHE, CROW, KIOWA, OMAHA, OSAGE, PAWNEE, SIOUX

Legendary creature of the Sioux-creator and keeper of the Earth

The Unktehi

The *unktehi* are gigantic, cow-like creatures originating in Sioux mythology. The males live in the water and are revered as grandfathers, while the females live in the Earth and are revered as grandmothers. Waterfalls in particular are considered holy places where the *unktehi* reside.

Besides their cow-like appearance, the *unktehi* have a very remarkable feature: their horns are forked. The veneration of the *unktehi* is the reason for the important place the buffalo holds in the Earth ceremonies of the Sioux tribes. It acquired this status due to its physical similarity to the *unktehi*. As a result, it represents the *unktehi* on the Earth.

The Dakota mythology links these truly gigantic creatures with the creation of the Earth. In the legend of the origin of their medicine hut, it says that *Wakan Tanka* (highest god) came down on a rainbow to the ancient sea, tore a rib out of his right side, and threw it into the sea. From this rib, the male *unktehi* came forth. In the same fashion, he created the female *unktehi* from a rib in his left side. After *Wakan Tanka* returned to the sky, both animals swam to the West, where they built the medicine hut on land that had suddenly emerged.

The ribs symbolize the semi-circles of the Earth's surface. The male and female *unktehi* travel around the Earth's halves and, thus, they represent the different sides of the Earth. The buffalo was later associated with this identity as well as being equated with woman and corn.

The enormous *unktehi*, whose tails and horns touch the sky, are constantly at war with the thunderbirds. The battles of the cosmic enemies are fought in thunderstorms and lightning, which often result in losses on both sides. This battle between Above and Below clearly shows the cosmic polarity in the way the Sioux views the world; it shows the duality of the world house.

Shaman symbol of the rain bringer

The Thunderbird

The thunderbird is a mythical being that is revered by all Native American tribes who live in the Plains. The picture on the opposite page shows it on a Dakota shield hanging between four stars and four bunches of feathers (the four cardinal points).

Native Americans regard the thunderbird as the rain bringer, as lightning flashes from its eyes and thunder is caused by the beating of its wings.

According to legend, the thunderbirds live in a cedar forest at the Western end of the world where they build their nests, wield cedar bats, and stuff their pipes with cedar needles. For this reason, cedar wood, which is only ever used in the war hut, is directly linked with the thunderbirds.

In a thunderstorm, the thunderbirds emerge and create the storm. The eagle, bird of the Sun, is regarded as the representative of the thunderbird in the Earthly realm.

Until this day, various tribes report sightings of the thunderbird. Every few years, a gigantic bird with a wing span of 66–83 feet, a white underside, and a black back is said to have flown over the land.

According to the beliefs of the Haida, a tribe in the Northwest of the United States, even a human soul can be transformed into a thunderbird.

Tobacco offerings were brought to the thunderbirds so that they would be kindly inclined toward man when man asked them for rain.

Sioux protective symbol for newborns

The Sacred Buffalo Skin

Mothers traditionally painted buffalo skins, similar to the one pictured on the opposite page, for the naming ceremony so that the newborn child received the protection of *Wakonda*.

The head and the front feet were dyed red to symbolize that part of the Earth from where the god would one day start his journey around the world. Red is the color of the new day and the time at which the mother rises to prepare food for her small child, whose young and tender life depends entirely on her efforts.

The thin line that runs from the head of the skin along the back represents the path of the day-god, who always travels from East to West. Halfway along this path is a red dot to represent the day-god at noon. Here, it marks the time at which the mother has to turn her thoughts away from other things and take care of feeding her child so that its life can continue.

The back feet and the tail are also dyed red to represent the glow which marks the end of the day when the day-god has reached the end of the Earth. This again turns the thoughts of the mother to the needs of her child.

If a woman paints these markings onto the buffalo skin, she will pray to *Wakonda* (the highest god of the Sioux, also known as *Wakan Tanka*) in her thoughts to ask his protection for herself and her child.

1.

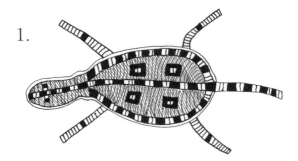

2.

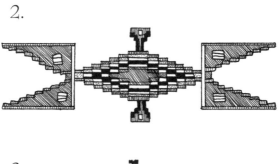

3.

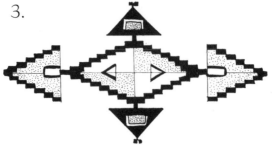

Sioux protective symbols for birth and small children

Tortoise Motifs of the Sioux

The tortoise's task is to lead the newborn safely into the world. In the Sioux's conception of the world, the tortoise is the carrier of the Earth and it, therefore, has a direct connection with birth and small children. Furthermore, it holds great significance as a figure in the cosmography.

The Central Algonquin and the Iroquois believe that the world rests on the back of an enormous turtle that brought about the world's beginning when it found its first firm foothold in the first ocean.

Mandan legends tell of the "Lonely Man" who was looking for the right skin for the sacred *okipa* drums and finally decided to use the shell of the turtles for this purpose. However, the turtles told him: "The world rests on our backs and, therefore, we four cannot leave from here." Instead, the man should craft the drums from buffalo skins and give them the shape of a turtle.

Figure 1 shows quite a realistic rendering of a tortoise. This was a little box made from leather where a baby's umbilical cord was kept.

Figures 2 and 3 show cosmic patterns of tortoises as found in decorations of cradles and women's leggings.

The Sioux were strictly against realistic depictions and any kinds of portraits. The European eye recognizes the shape of the tortoise with some difficulty in Figures 2 and 3, and regards them as a symbol composed of triangles, rectangles, and diamonds. For the Sioux, however, Figures 2 and 3 represent reality as they see it.

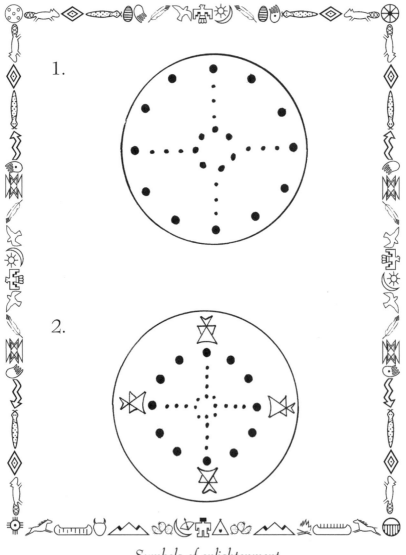

Symbols of enlightenment

Sioux Medicine Wheels

Figure 1 shows a medicine wheel in its most simple form by using stones arranged on the ground. There are seven stones in the middle to represent the seven stars or seven arrows and, thus, the seven types of human and universal personality. They can symbolize fear, courage, love, or sorrow. The other meanings are left to the imagination of the individuals, since this is part of the learning process. Seven arrows always stand for the true nature of a person.

Every stone in the big medicine wheel represents a person, animal, plant, or something else, and each is regarded as having equal value.

The gifts of medicine are now multiplied by the four main directions that are also contained in the symbolism of the wheel. Seven plus four equals eleven, and the eleven is then quadrupled to make forty-four, which represents the forty-four great shields of the medicine chiefs, the men of peace. These gifts are meant to enrich man's life so that he will grow and learn.

Figure 2 displays the additional feature of eagle tents at each of the four cardinal points. When people are born into this world, they always come along one of these four paths. This medicine wheel refers to those who are born with the medicine—that is, the power—of the eagles. After they have gone beyond the age of 9, they will start to experience this energy.

If a person is born as a yellow eagle, it means he has the far sight of the East. If he is an eagle of the South, however, he will also see far but with innocence of heart, which is indicated by the color green. The black eagle of the West will see far, but more from an introspective point of view. If he wears the white cloak of the North, his ability to see far will focus more on the realms of knowledge.

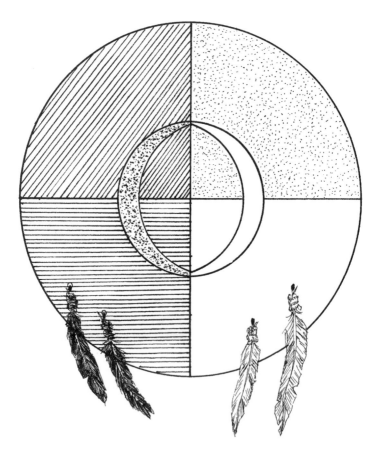

Symbol of the universe

Sioux Medicine Shield

This shield is painted in blue, green, red, and yellow. The color blue represents the cedar of the holy mountains and stands for prayer. The color green stands for innocence of heart. The color red represents the campfires of the people and spirit. Yellow stands for the eagle of the East, because man has to be able to see far in order to recognize things. This shield, as a whole, embodies the universe.

The feathers that are fastened to the shield, two red and two black falcon's feathers, symbolize the "Falcon-who-sees-by-day" and the "Falcon-who-sees-by-night." The quills of the feathers are bound with black otter fur and white mink fur. These are symbols of wisdom, introspection, and the healing powers of the medicine man. The playfulness of these animals signals that the people, too, should play like children in the medicine water.

The half Moon shapes that are facing each other symbolize twins, the duality of man, which is similar to the symbol of the split pole. Therefore, while man stands in the light, he can only see one half of the shield and has to look for the other one in the darkness where there is fear, but also joy. One of the half Moons stands for one's own personality, whereas the other one stands for other people. As a result, everyone is a mirror for the other and they are, therefore, one. For this reason, this representation is regarded as the shield of "Two's Moon," indicating that the two Moons in reality are one. "Two's Moon" is one of the forty-four medicine chiefs.

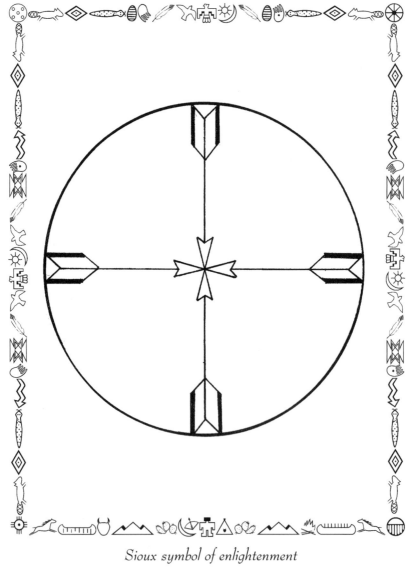

Sioux symbol of enlightenment

The Four Medicine Arrows

The shield shown on the opposite page depicts the sign of the four medicine arrows. These arrows contain teachings about man. Every story and every situation should be regarded from the four different directions and judged accordingly.

From the direction of wisdom: the North arrow.

From the direction of innocence: the South arrow.

From the direction of far sight: the East arrow.

From the direction of introspection: the West arrow.

This medicine wheel, thus, shows people a way to learn more about themselves, their brothers, the world, and the universe.

Because of the different ways of looking at things, the meaning of a story or an event unfolds little by little like the flower at the center of the symbol. Formed by the four arrows, the flower also indicates that all events and stories are, after all, one, because all four arrows of enlightenment join up in the center.

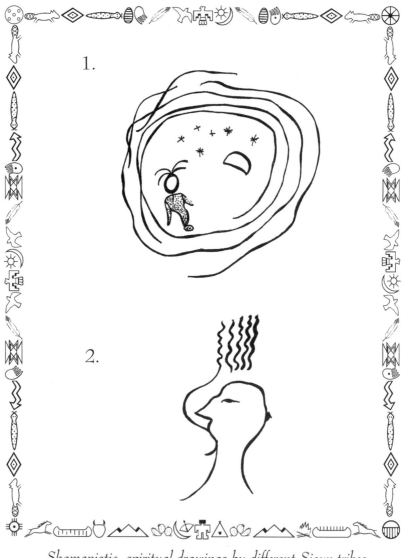

1.

2.

Shamanistic, spiritual drawings by different Sioux tribes

Ojibwa Engravings on Birch Tree Bark

Figure 1 shows an Ojibwa shaman who has received the power to reach the sky through being a member of the Great Medicine Society (the *midewiwin*). This power is represented by the lines that emanate from his head. The sky above him is cloudless and allows an unrestricted view of the Moon and stars. According to Ojibwa beliefs, there are several skies, one on top of the other. This belief is represented in the engraving by several concentric circles.

Oglala (Lakota Sioux) Drawing on Animal Skin

Figure 2 shows a man who possesses the power of the wakan. He is lifting his right arm, and from his fingers radiates the energy of the wakan, which is represented by wavy lines. This is a classic depiction of the wakan gesture. This drawing shows a wicasa wakan, which means approximately the same as medicine man. He rules over the wakan beings.

The name *wakan* is difficult to explain. It can probably be best described as the spirit of all beings and things. There are good and evil *wakan* beings, which can be called upon and invoked by man. However, all *wakan* beings are ultimately one, which is referred to as *Wakan Tanka* (great mystery).

A priest's most important possession is his *wasikun*, his medicine pouch. However, this description is misleading, as the pouch does not contain medicine. Instead, it holds a powerful *wakan* being, which lends great powers to the priest.

1.

2.

Standards of war

Osage Standards

The two figures on the opposite page show crooks around which a swan's skin has been wound eight times. The two crooks together represent the cosmos in its entirety.

The standard that represents the sky is adorned with the feathers of an adult golden eagle. They are pure white with black tips (Figure 1). The standard that represents the Earth, on the other hand, is decorated with the feathers of a young bird that is not yet fully grown (Figure 2). A small wreath made of eagle's down is fastened to the bottom ends of the two standards. Swan's skins have been wound around the crooks eight times in which four rotations stand for one half of the cosmos.

The peace pipe as a symbol of the cosmos

Sioux Peace Pipe

The pipe shown on the opposite page is made of the wood of the ash tree and is about 7 spans long. The mouthpiece is decorated with a collar of iridescent duck feathers and a woodpecker's head. In the middle, there are collars made from owl feathers, and the bottom end is covered by the neck and head of a mallard, fastened with red leather thongs. The top section of the pipe is decorated with three strands of horsehair, which are dyed red and fastened with white cords. The bottom end of the pipe is adorned with an open fan of feathers from a golden eagle. The ten feathers are white with black tips and have been taken from the tail of an adult bird. A handful of down feathers has been tied to the bottom end of the fan. The pipe shaft is painted blue and, thus, represents the male side of the world, the sky, and the North. The red strands of horsehair are symbolic of the rays of the Sun, while the white cords represent the moonlight. Night is embodied by the owl feathers, day by the woodpecker. Both of them together stand for death and life. Warriors are likened to the white feathers of the golden eagle.

There exists a female counterpart to this pipe. The female pipe belongs to the women and is constructed in the same way as the male pipe. However, the fan at the end of the pipe is made from seven tail feathers of a young eagle, which are dark colored and marked with numerous dots. The pipe shaft is painted green, which refers to the female half of the cosmos, the Earth's cloak, and the South.

Thus, the two pipes embrace the entire cosmos. Both together are sacred cult objects of the Sioux.

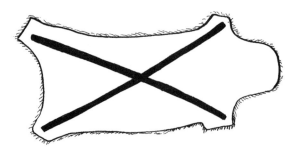

Shamanistic ritual designed to retain the Earth's favor

Patterns for the Sacred White Buffalo Skin

If a hunter were so lucky as to kill one of the rare white buffalo, the slain animal would be subjected to a long ritual ceremony where even the smallest details were predetermined. The hunter would only be allowed to keep the animal if he had four sons; otherwise, he was forced to sell it. If he fulfilled this prerequisite, he would ask a virgin to clean the animal's skin. The girl would receive two complete sets of new clothing and a horse for this work.

The skin would be laid out to dry inside the tent, on the West side, and would constantly be guarded. Afterwards, it would be spread out on a new blanket, with its head facing East. The girl would then make a cross shown in the top figure on the opposite page. This cross symbolizes the four winds and the four cardinal points of the Earth. The priest would then turn the skin and paint a number of red circles onto the fur between the shoulders. The innermost circle would be divided up by a cross. During this process, the priest would pray to the sky, the Earth, and to all things that grow.

The buffalo skin and the buffalo's skull, also painted with concentric circles, were then laid out in two specially prepared squares (5 feet × 5 feet) from which all the grass had been removed. Only the bare ground can receive prayers and speeches properly. The skin was placed with the fur facing up and the head end pointing toward the pole at the center of the village. Then an extremely complex and lengthy ritual ensued in which every move and word were prescribed in detail. Any mistakes made during the proceedings were regarded as a great misfortune that could not be easily compensated.

The ritual closed with the white buffalo skin being cut into ribbons and handed out to the guests, who would keep them throughout their lives. They would be worn around the head at many festive occasions, but never during war or in battle.

151

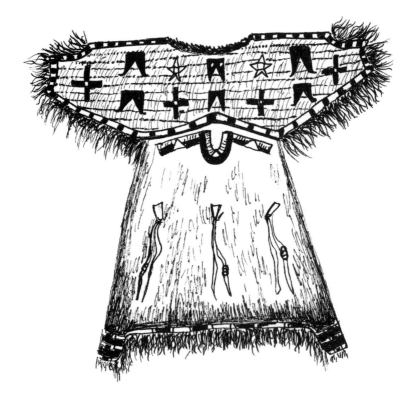

Symbolism reflected in Sioux clothing

A Decorated Woman's Shirt

The figure on the opposite page shows a woman's shirt decorated in typical Sioux style. It is a leather shirt in which the neck and shoulders are decorated with colorful patterns. The shirt is embroidered with blue glass beads, which represent an area of water according to Native American beliefs. The embroidered symbols represent stars and clouds, which are reflected in the water. This part of the garment is framed by the seashore, which is symbolized by the dark and light band. The U-symbol below it stands for the tortoise.

On the one hand, the tortoise symbol refers to the myth of the carrier of the Earth; on the other hand, it also plays an important part as a birth symbol. For example, the umbilical cord was kept in a tortoise-shaped container, and cradles or women's leggings were often decorated with tortoise motifs.

*Headdress made of eagles' feathers: Symbol of a
direct connection to the highest god*

Feather Crown of the Crow

Among the Sioux tribes, a feather headdress was part of the festive garb of a noble person. For a classic headdress, twenty-eight eagle feathers would be inserted into bone cases and fastened to a strong ribbon (in this case, a red and blue patterned ribbon). The number twenty-eight is considered sacred, because the Moon lives for twenty-eight days and the buffalo has twenty-eight ribs.

Apart from the example shown on the opposite page, there existed a kind of crown that was worn as a sign of distinction by the chief. It had the additional feature of long, train-like extensions, which were set with feathers and reached to the ground.

When honoring the highest god, *Wakan Tanka*, all Sioux tribes also display a certain reverence for altitude. Thus, they prayed high up on cliffs and mountains, where they believed themselves to be closer to the sky. For that reason, these locations were also often chosen for fasting.

As the eagle is able to fly highest of all living creatures, it is sometimes thought of as the embodiment of *Wakan Tanka*. It is always considered as a mediator between the god and the people. According to the legends, it was the golden eagle that led the people from the world of stars down to their Earthly existence.

Hunting the golden eagle was considered a sacred act and one of the objectives was to obtain the twelve tail feathers, since they represented the rays of the Sun and the number of months in a year. It should be noted that the Sioux thought in terms of a year having twelve months.

The feathers making up the eagles' feather headdress reflect the corona of the Sun and frame the head of the wearer with something akin to the aura of the Sun.

155

Ritual dance shield

Teton Shield Painting

On the Teton dance shield shown on the opposite page, the buffalo head is placed at the center of the rectangle that represents the Earth. This, in turn, is framed by the circle, which the shield forms. The circle symbolizes unity and the Earth so that the buffalo are enclosed by the rim of the Earth.

It is likely that originally all Sioux tribes East of the Mississippi were stag hunters and only turned to hunting buffalo as they slowly advanced into the plains. As a result, the buffalo took the place that the stag held in rituals and, thus, took over its relationship with the Earth.

The original legends of the Osage hold that the buffalo belongs to the latecomers that need to attract attention through roaring, if they want to be accepted into the society of the *gentes* (see p. 159).

The buffalo came to be associated with the number four, which is the Earth's number, and with the most important fruits of the field. In ceremonies, the buffalo is equivalent to woman. By and by the buffalo was linked more closely with the symbolism of the Earth—a development that was certainly supported by the fact that the *unktehi* (p. 131) had been revered all along, long before the buffalo appeared on the scene.

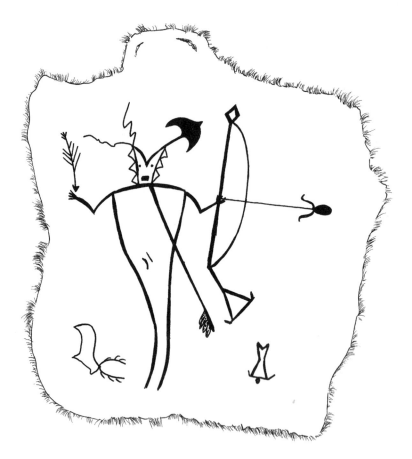

The unnatural god of contradictory behavior

The Giant Haokah

The giant *Haokah* is a central figure of Native American belief. His cult was widespread among all Sioux tribes. The depiction on the opposite page is based on a drawing dating from 1845 by a Sioux warrior.

In his left hand, *Haokah* holds his symbol, the lance of contradiction. He is also referred to as the unnatural god, and all Sioux tribes regard him as the ruler of dreams. One side of *Haokah*'s face is red, the other is blue. His eyes, too, are of different colors. During winter, he suffers from great heat; during summer, he feels cold. Hot water to him feels cold and cold water hot. This is why the *Haokah* cult demands of its members to immerse their hands in boiling water and drink boiling hot broth, all the while proclaiming how nice and cool these are.

To this day, such ceremonies take place in honor of this giant. They are conducted by people who have experienced dreams similar to those of their mythical role model. They display all types of behavior that emphasize the contradictory character of the god. There are, for instance, the capers of bad manners, talking backwards, shaving only half their head, etc. If a member of the *Haokah* cult is asked to go away, he will instead come closer. The followers of *Haokah*, however, never formed a substantial grouping; they were usually just a few individuals, never more than two or three per tribe.

Symbol of honor of the Osage and Omaha

Traditional Spider Symbol

This motif is common among the Osage and the Omaha. It is one of the symbols of life of the *Honga Utanondsi* and would appear as a tattoo on the back of the hand of an honored woman. It combines the *tsi wakondagi* (the cross in the middle) with the spider cross. Both represent the same archetype and symbolize the Earth.

The Osage myth of origin tells of twenty-one *gentes* coming down from heaven (the tribe is the cosmos and the *gentes* are its parts). After wandering the Earth for a long time in search of life, they came to a strange village that was surrounded by bleached human and animal bones. This was the village of death where the *Honga Utanondsi*, who used the four winds to kill all living beings, lived. Now, however, they joined the *gentes* and abandoned their murderous ways. For this, they received the *tsi wakondagi*, the house of mysteries. This house represents the life-giving Earth, just as the *Honga Utanondsi* themselves represent the Earth.

Honga means "sacred object" and *utanondsi* means "an object separated from all other things"—thus referring to the Earth, which is separated from the *honga* of the sky: the Sun, the Moon, the morning and evening stars, Ursa Major, and the Pleiades.

Newborn babies were brought into this world house of the "isolated" *honga* to receive the sacred food of life to assure them of a long life. Furthermore, this was where they received their tribal names.

The symbols of the *Honga Utanondsi* unite the polarities of life and death. Thus, all four types of snakes that are assigned to them (adder, buffalo snake, black snake, and rattlesnake) stand for rebirth, because, according to the legend, all four snakes declare: "Even if the people enter the realm of the ghosts, they should regain life and consciousness through the use of my teeth."

Shamanic symbol of dualism used by various tribes of the Plains

The Forked Tree

The forked tree symbolizes division among humans. People tend to feel that it is always the other one who does not understand or who is wrong. This "other one" is represented in the forked tree. The tree is split in two, but still forms a unit. Both sides look exactly the same and end in branches and leaves, which are also exactly identical. One side is always a reflection of the other side. Of course, the question arises: Which side represents the onlooker, which side is the observed? Or is he both? Every person is reflected in other people.

The forked tree is also symbolic of the inner conflict within a person. One half of that person can love, while the other half is capable of hatred. It is important that both sides understand each other; otherwise that person would just be torn apart. The same holds true for different ethnic groups. they also have to try to understand each other; otherwise death and destruction will ensue. If one half of the tree tries to separate from the other, the tree will become stunted or it will die.

Native American understanding does not regard good and evil as two separate forces, but rather as two aspects that make up a whole. These seemingly contradictory powers can be found in the forked tree. It is important to try to join these apparent contradictions in human nature with the one universe.

The forked tree is a very common symbol that is used by many tribes, but holds special significance for the tribes of the Plains.

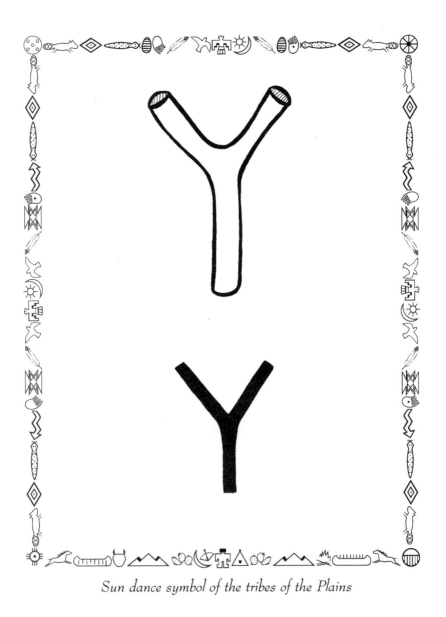

Sun dance symbol of the tribes of the Plains

The Forked Stake

Forked stakes represent human beings and embody their twin-like existence. Smaller forked stakes can also stand for everything else in this world. They are free of judgment, as one twin is always reflected in the other, but ultimately they are both one.

Forked stakes are used for a number of rituals. During the Sun dance of the Plains tribes, for example, twelve stakes are placed around a forked tree. The twelve stakes represent the twelve great nations on the Earth, while the tree in the middle points out the unity of all people.

Like the forked tree, the stake is a symbol shared by various tribes, but it is of particular importance to the tribes of the Plains.

Typical depiction of a cosmic dream that is common to several tribes

Tepee Paintings by the Cree Tribes of the Plains

The drawing on the opposite page shows the frequently recurring depiction of a cosmic dream that can be found in an almost identical fashion among the Ojibwa, Algonquin, Fox, and Arapaho.

It describes the path of the dreamer (1) that leads him to a rectangle that is half red and half black, which represents the Earth. Above him, the sky arches, decked with the Moon and the stars (2). The dreamer slips further away along the road to the *manitu*'s home (3) and finally reaches a ring with three spikes (the fourth spike is obscured by the path), which again represents the Earth. From there, he looks down on the world below that is divided by two rainbows. One spans from North to South, the other spans from East to West. If he raises his eyes upward, he can see the Sun, the morning star, and birds of all kinds.

The path of the visionary, however, continues much higher to the place from where *manitu* (here, marked by a circle with four red dots) has sent forth the four winds (4). All areas that have vertical hatching in this drawing are painted red.

The dream catcher protects against bad dreams

Dream Catcher

Originally, the dream catcher was used by the Canadian and the North American Sioux and the Ojibwa. It is hung above the bed to filter out bad dreams and thoughts, which need to disappear by the next morning. The good dreams, however, find their way through the net and travel down the pendulum.

The tradition of the dream catcher can be traced back to a Sioux woman whose child was tortured by nightmares. As she could see no other way out, she went and asked the old spider woman for advice. She was told to fashion an eternal circle out of willow branches and weave the net of life with cotton threads. Ever since, the dream catcher's purpose has been to help people enjoy their dreams and life.

The drawing on the opposite page shows a dream catcher in which the ring has been wound with leather. A pendulum made of feathers and beads is fastened to both sides and to the lowest point of the ring. The net of the dream catcher can take different shapes. In addition to the design shown in this drawing, spiral designs are also commonly found.

1.

2. 3. 4.

5.

6. 7. 8.

Horse decorations

Horse Decorations

It was common among the tribes of the Plains for both horse and rider to wear painted symbols. Some of these can be seen on the opposite page:

1. The symbol on the croup of the horse indicates that the rider has killed one or more enemies in battle.

2. This marking identifies the leader of a war party.

3. The circle means that the rider fought behind a chest shield.

4. This symbol shows that horses were among the spoils.

5. This is a medicine symbol.

6. A symbol of grief.

7. The symbol of hail.

8. The symbol of a coup.

Such painted symbols served as identification during battle or the hunt. They also provided information about the deeds and the emotional state of the bearer.

A shield for protection and erecting boundaries

Personal Medicine Shield

The shield shown on the opposite page was made by a member of the Crow. Its body is made up of buffalo skin painted with bird motifs. Additionally, two ermine pelts and a bundle of feathers are fastened to the shield with strings. At the lower edge, the shield is hemmed with a red ribbon to which eagle's feathers have been tied. Red ribbons with the feathers from different birds are fastened to both sides of the shield. The shield itself is gray in color.

On a level that cannot be perceived by others, a medicine shield reflects what is essential to the inner self of its bearer and what his will is. It can represent past experiences or the next hurdle that its owner will have to clear. It always shows all the events and talents that its bearer would like to experience and develop during the course of his life. He consciously distances himself away from all other experiences that are outside the shield's boundaries. The outline of the shield, therefore, forms a boundary that protects the bearer from unwanted events.

Women made their own shields that reflected their personalities and showed off their abilities. Men used to choose a brother whom they respected to create their shields so that the male ego would not embellish the truth. It was considered a great wrong-doing to lie about one's abilities and it could lead to expulsion from the community of the tribe. Shields that told untruths would be burnt in a ceremony of mourning.

Medicine shields were also made for specific ceremonies and as a good luck charm.

The simplest way to make one's own shield is to draw a circle onto a piece of paper and inscribe it with all the events and circumstances one wishes for in one's life. This will attract joyful events and keep unwanted circumstances at a distance.

173

5

Northwest Coast

COOS, HAIDA, KWAKIUTL, SALISH, TLINGIT

1.

2.

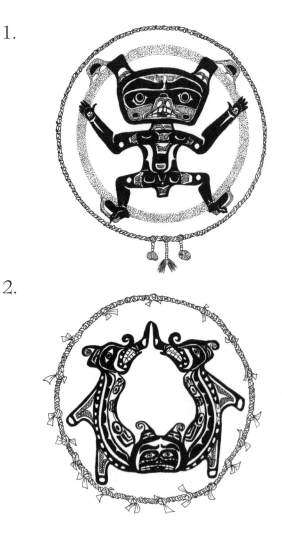

Clan emblems of the Kwakiutl

Grizzly Bear in the Sun

Figure 1 shows a motif of the Kwakiutl, a Native American tribe of the Pacific Northwest. It represents the bear which, like the salmon, stands for strength and food. Such coats of arms or clan emblems were and are used to decorate the house as well as all kinds of domestic items, and for the making of totem poles and other ritual objects.

The reason why certain clans feel an affiliation with certain animals can be found in mythology: In the beginning, there were no other living beings apart from *Alkuntam*, the highest deity, who lived in *Nusmatta*. One day, he decided to populate the world and created the four supernatural carpenters who invented work and carved the earliest ancestors from wood. They also carved and painted all animals, birds, trees, flowers, mountains, rivers, and stars—all living beings apart from the Sun, which already existed.

On the walls of *Nusmatta*, the costumes of different animals and birds were hung, and the creator invited the ancestors to wear these. Each chose the animal he or she liked best. *Alkuntam* then named them and sent them to the Earth, where every animal landed on a mountaintop. There, the ancestors took off their costumes and assumed human shape. The animal costumes floated back up to *Nusmatta*.

The clans of the Northwest trace back their origin to legends like these. They consider it their right to bear the animal in their coat of arms in whose shape their first ancestor came to Earth.

The Snake of the Kwakiutl

Figure 2 shows the snake in its human and animal form.

Shaman's costume for the Kwakiutl winter dance

Thunderbird Costume with Mask

The costume shown on the opposite page has its origins in the Kwakiutl tradition. It consists of two main figures: the thunderbird and the *bokwo*, the wild man of the woods.

The tribes of the Northwest coast have over time developed a highly complex system of ceremonies. The Wakash tribes, in particular, used the winter to stage dramatic rituals and dances. However, only the nobility could afford to participate in these rituals with the required pomp, because they were always preceded by a *potlach*, a ritual exchange of gifts in which the clan chiefs tried to outdo each other with their generosity.

The story behind the winter dance was that somebody had been abducted by a supernatural being, such as the *bokwo*, the spirit of the grizzly bear, or the man-eater *Pápakalanósiwa*. The being would transfer its own wild character onto that person, who would then need to be saved in a ritual and tamed until he could rejoin normal society. In reality, the victim was a novice who was inducted into the secrets of the winter dance.

1.

2.

The raven as bringer of light and food

The Theft of the Sun

In the Kwakiutl drawing on the opposite page (Fig. 1), the raven sets free the Sun, which he has carried down to Earth. The raven is a typical "creature of change" in the legends of the Northwestern tribes.

When darkness still reigned over the world and animal creatures lived in a town at the Southern tip of the Queen Charlotte Islands, the son of the chief took ill one day and died. One morning, in the high bed where her son's body had lain, the mother found a young man with a body blazing like fire. She soon started to worry about the radiant young man, because he had no appetite and refused to eat. One day, however, the boy observed two slaves who ate large amounts of food. The male slave gave the boy a little scab from his leg to eat together with some whale meat. The young boy then proceeded to eat until he had devoured all the supplies of the village. The chief was horrified and called for the boy. He gave him the feather costume of the raven and called him *wigyét* (giant). He also handed him a pouch filled with seed, asking him to fly to the mainland and sow the seed.

After the *wigyét* had sown fish eggs and berries, he thought that it would be easier to find food if the world no longer lay in darkness. Knowing that the light was kept in the sky, he flew up through the clouds where he met the daughter of the sky chief. Immediately, he assumed the shape of a cedar leaf, which she swallowed and from which she became pregnant. Consequently, he was reborn in the house of the sky chief and was able to steal the daylight that was kept in a box hanging from the ceiling. When he returned to the Earth, he broke the box open and filled the world with light.

Figure 2 shows the sleeping pole of the raven, which is owned by the Tsimshian chief *Quawm* in British Columbia. The human figures are called "surrounding people," or "children," and are a frequent feature in Tsimshian totem poles.

181

*Shamanistic depiction of the Tlingit salmon in both
its animal and human form.*

The Salmon According to Tlingit Legends

According to Native American thinking, all creatures brought forth by nature are required to be treated with respect. The tribes of the Pacific Northwest believe that there is a strong spiritual link with the salmon. This animal was once as important for survival as corn was for the tribes in the Southwest of the United States.

According to the belief of the tribes in the Northwest, the salmon people live in a village in the sea. Even salmon that has been eaten and now exists in the spiritual world will reassume the human body in their village, provided that the people who caught and ate the salmon have thrown the bones and eyes of the fish back into the water. Only in this way is the continued existence of these creatures guaranteed.

The salmon has always been attributed with magical abilities. Salmon can change into human beings and vice versa. A person that has changed into a salmon and back again returns as a particularly powerful shaman.

The picture on the opposite page shows a shamanistic depiction of the salmon according to the Tlingit legends. Both the soul of the salmon and the human body have been captured in this drawing.

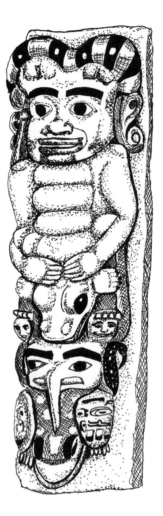

Pole carrying the coat of arms of the Tlingit Woodworm Clan

Tlingit Totem Pole

This totem or heraldic pole comes from the whale house of the Tlingit in Kluckwan, Alaska, where it was used as a post in the house. It shows the coat of arms of the Woodworm Clan.

The upper section of the pole shows a human face and arms. The lower body then changes into the shape of the woodworm. Some house spirits have been incorporated to the left and right of it. In the lower section, the spirit of the worm can be found with protective clan shields to its left and right.

Tlingit history of the Woodworm Clan's coat of arms tells of a chief's daughter who secretly kept a woodworm, which she fed with oil until it had grown as long as an arm. She only appeared for meals and disappeared again straight afterwards. People heard her singing at night. Once, her mother followed her and saw something large and terrible between the storage boxes, but because she knew that her daughter was fond of the creature, she left it in peace. Then the people in the village started missing the oil that had been fed to the worm and decided to kill it. They asked the girl to leave her room. She initially refused but finally came out. After she was told that her "son" was dead, she started to sing. From this time on, the songs of the chief's daughter were sung by the Ganatedi clan, and the woodworm became their heraldic beast.

Stories about the woodworm are very common along the Pacific Coast. The Achomavi in Northern California tell the story that the woodworm is a shy, but handsome young man. The Coos in Oregon tell of a young woman who gave shelter to a grub, which developed into a terrifying snake. But this beloved pet continued to bring so much food that the family became very wealthy.

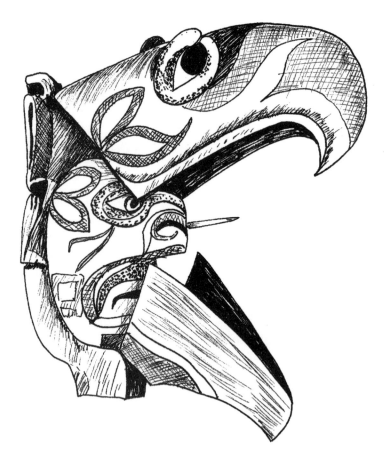

Haida transformation mask

Haida Thunderbird Mask

The Haida live on the Northwest coast of North America. The drawing on the opposite page shows a mask carved out of wood, which was made by the Haida for use in shamanistic rituals. The mask represents the head of a thunderbird and, when opened, reveals a human face.

The Haida believe that the human spirit can assume the shape of a thunderbird—a mythological creature common to many Native American tribes. The thunderbird brings rain and thunderstorms and is, thus, responsible for the growth of plants and the preservation of life on Earth.

The fall of Mu

The Final Destruction of the Legendary Motherland

The drawing on the opposite page originates with the Nootkas who live in British Columbia, in Southwestern Canada. As far as we know, it is the only drawing ever created on the subject by a Native American tribe. It contains information about the disaster that many thousands of years ago completely destroyed the motherland Mu, the home to which all Native Americans trace back their origins.

The wave-like body of the embellished snake describes the waves of the ocean. The sea is represented by the whale, and the shallower water is represented by the wavy line in its mouth. In the eyes of all native tribes of the Pacific Northwest, the killer whale is symbolic of the ocean. It is also called the "Great Murderer," because the ocean once flooded the land of Mu and drowned millions of people.

In the middle, between the whale and the snake, is the thunderbird. It was a common symbol in the motherland and it carried out the seven orders of the four original creative powers. In this drawing, the thunderbird digs its talons into the whale's back, which means that the four great powers have complete control over everything the water does.

The whale's neck is broken. The U-shaped symbol comes from the alphabet of the priests and stands for the abyss into which the motherland was drawn. The four white dots along its spine and the four wavy lines below again point to the four great powers. Above the spine are five wavy lines, including the highest, the creator god.

The eye of the "Great Murderer" consists of three concentric squares. The two outer lines stand for the mother and the land while the square in the middle represents darkness. This part of the drawing thus reads: "The motherland was drawn into the abyss of darkness."

189

6

The Subarctic Region

BEAVER, CHIPEWYAN, CREE, NASKAPI (INNU), OJIBWA, SAULTEAUX

Dream visions of home among the Northern tribes

The Double Curve

The motif of the double curve is one of the most prominent features in Native American art of the North. In its simplest shape, it consists of a line with both ends bent toward each other. It is found in artworks of the Naskapi, Micmac, Malecite, Passamaquoddy, and Penobscot. The two examples shown on the opposite page were created by the Penobscot. The double curve is most common in the Northeastern region between the Hudson Bay and Kennebec. Outside these regions, toward the West and the South, the symbol changes and may even become a rather naturalistic picture with leaves and flowers. This increasing naturalism can probably be traced back to European influences, such as the French flower style of the 17th and 18th centuries.

The Penobscot called the original version *elawikhazik*, which means a "written symbol." The typical Nordic pattern is always shown with the motif of a rising tree, which emerges from the center of the curve and is often symbolized by long leaves.

Regrettably, the meaning of the double curve has been more or less lost. The Montagnais and the Naskapi recognize depictions of dream visions in these patterns.

It is, however, safe to say that the double curve can be associated with the myth of *Tshikápis*—a heroic figure who never grew any taller than a baby. After the murder of his parents, his sister took him from his mother's womb and raised him, although he had not yet been due to be born. After he had eradicated the last monster on Earth and tied the Sun and the Moon with ropes, he and his family climbed an enormous tree and, from there, moved to the realm where they now live.

The bottom picture on the opposite page carries a more detailed description: "Wigwam in the middle of a valley between two wooded hills, with the Sun above; day and night to the left and right."

The world order according to the Ojibwa

Ojibwa Logogram in Del Ashkewe

The top symbol stands for the creator, *Kitche Manitu*. A circle on its own means "spirit" (page 25). For it to become a "Great Spirit," an outer circle is added along with four spikes that indicate omnipresence.

The half circle, which is opened at the bottom, represents the sky and the universe. The symbol of the Sun underneath it, with its linear extensions, represents life and time.

Below the Sun is the depiction of a man in a circle, representing human existence. This symbol is connected through the lifeline with the symbol of the creator.

The two semi-circular lines coming off the symbol of human existence represent the tree of life, the plant world, on which all other living beings depend.

The horizontal line is the basis of the lifeline and stands for the Earth and stones. The tepees on this horizontal line have different shapes to indicate different ways of life. The Sun and the Moon can be found to the left and the right of this line.

The two men next to the figure in the circle show wavy lines emerging from their mouths. These represent language, history, and stories. The figures of women next to them are symbolic of continuity and naturalness of the female element. The two figures on the outside represent the provider. The four main animals together with the humans, the tree of life, and the Earth represent existence and time.

A mythical dream

Drawing of an Ojibwa Woman's Dream

The drawing on the opposite page represents a visionary dream. Catherine Wabose of the Ojibwa tribe had the following vision during a childhood fast:

After a voice had called to her, she followed a narrow, glowing path (1) that resembled a silver thread. When she stopped after a short while and turned to the right, she saw the new Moon and a flame on the summit (2); when she turned to the left, she saw the sinking Sun (3). After walking on a little further, she saw on the right the face of the "Always Standing Woman" (4), who introduced herself and told her that she would give her immortality and her name. She also informed her that she would have a long life on Earth and the gift to save the lives of others. The dreamer then walked on and soon encountered a man with a circular body, from whose head semi-circular rays were emanating (5). He introduced himself as the "Little Man Spirit" and instructed her to give this name to her first son, as this was his life. She then followed the path as far as an opening in the sky (7) where she was called by a man whose chest was covered by rectangles and whose head was surrounded by a strong glow (6). He introduced himself as the "Radiant Blue Sky" and promised her to equip her with the gifts of life so that she would be able to resist and endure. As he said this, glowing arrowheads came toward her and fell down at her feet (8). The spirit then told her to climb onto a fish-like being, which swam through the air and took her back at incredible speed so that her hair was billowing behind her (9). Immediately after her return, Catherine's vision ended.

All the beings that Catherine encountered in her dream are characters from her people's mythology. They belong to a very old group of myths, which is in danger of being lost. There is always a certain continuity in Native American visions when it comes to mythological images.

The highest god as the core of the psyche

Naskapi Representation of the Highest Being

In the mythology of the earlier cultures, the circle symbolizes the self or the whole. The Naskapi often represent the "Big Man" in the shape of a Mandala instead of a human figure. In the drawing on the opposite page, the black figure at the center of the circle represents the core of the soul of all beings. The figure is surrounded by a stylized snake, which is responsible for change and renewal.

The zigzagging bands in the outer circle stand for the ability to learn. The pointed features of these motifs indicate a connection between the individual points of view.

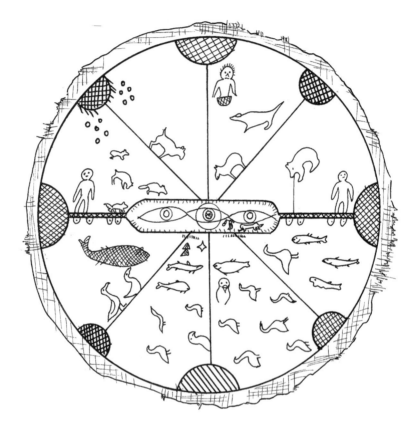

Multilayered depiction of world order

The World as Seen By the Ojibwa

The drawing on the opposite page shows *aki*, the circle that is the world with its four main and four secondary directions along the edge and the medicine hut at the center.

North, South, East, and West are represented by the four main directions, while the four secondary directions stand for the Northeast wind, the Northwest wind, the Southeast wind and the Southwest wind, among others. They also point out the summer and winter solstices and the autumn and spring equinoxes. The four quarters that have been created by the four main directions are further divided into a male and a female half. To these eight segments of the world circle, animals were added that correspond to the points of the compass and to the seasons. We can see here a very complex rendering of the world order.

At the center of the drawing is the medicine hut of the people, which was erected in honor of the creator god. According to general belief, the Great *Manitu* sat on the roof during the medicine ritual, listening to the beats of the water drum, smelling the scent of the tobacco offering, and rejoicing in the songs that were sung in his honor.

Shamanistic painted decoration of a drum, intended to allow access to other worlds

Painted Drum Belonging to a Beaver Shaman

The painting shows the outer world of the four winds and the two inner, supernatural worlds.

According to the Beaver myth of creation, the creator god *Yagesati* (He-who-is-motionless-in-the-sky) drew a cross onto the original sea. This determined the characteristics of the Earth. Horizontally, it set out the four cardinal points, and, vertically, it became the connecting element between the upper and the lower worlds.

The painting on the opposite page shows the cross and the paths that lead to the supernatural realms at its center. The painting also represents the characteristics that are associated with the four winds:

East = Sunrise, birth, red (the blood of birth), spring, male, good

South = Midday, infancy, yellow, summer, female, good

West = Sunset, childhood, red (the blood of menstruation), fall, female, dangerous

North = Night, puberty (time for initiation), white, winter, male, dangerous

The Beaver regards the cycle of the seasons as lasting 2 years. There is the cold year, which consists of fall and winter, and the warm year, which is made up of spring and summer. During the cold seasons, the male aspect prevails over the female, and during the warm seasons, the female aspect prevails over the male. Each half requires the other as a counterbalance and possesses traits of the other half. Thus, nights also exist during summer and days exist during the winter.

Shamanistic representation of a manitu

Ojibwa Drawing on Birch Bark

This drawing is the pictorial representation of a Midewiwin song that says, "When the waters are calm and the fogs lift, I will appear from time to time." The circle represents the sky filled with moisture and clouds. From it, rises the face of a *manitu*.

Today, the term *manitu* is used more or less as equivalent to the god of Christianity. Originally, however, it stood for the spirit or essence of a being or object. It can appear in the shape of an animal, human, or as an impersonal power. If, for example, the steam in a steam bath is regarded as *manitu*, it is because it is considered to be a spirit that has temporarily been transformed into steam. If a tobacco offering is made to a peculiar-looking object, it is because this object either belongs to a spirit or is temporarily inhabited by one. The term *manitu* can, therefore, also stand for something powerful, peculiar, or noteworthy.

1.

2.

Ojibwa spiritual drawings on birch bark

Midewiwin Engravings

Figure 1 shows a member of the *midewiwin*, the great medicine society of the Ojibwa. He is currently experiencing the holy state of *manitu*. The lines, which lead to his ears from below, indicate that he has been initiated into the secret knowledge of the Earth. His knowledge of the holy beings of the sky is indicated by the lines that lead down to his ears from above.

The prerequisite for reaching such a holy state is and always has been an immediate experience of another world. It is still expected of Native American boys and girls to use fasting and various ceremonies as a means of searching for visions. Young people will only be considered as adults once they have received a vision.

A particularly powerful vision can result in a person becoming the manifestation of the sacredness of another world.

The *midewiwin* illustration in Figure 2 shows the path of life from youth (left) to old age (right). The seven turnoffs where the path curves represent the seven temptations that man has to resist during the course of his life. If he succeeds, he will live to a great old age; if he leaves the path, he may, according to the views of the *midewiwin*, meet disease or even death.

Ornamental decorations

Painted Blanket

The original blanket that is shown on the opposite page can be found in the Denver Art Museum. It is said to be a piece of work by the Naskapi.

The material is made of plant fibers. This work shows an extraordinary combination of different symbols, for example, the motif of the feather headdress of the Plains (at the center) uniting with decorations that are typically subarctic in origin, i.e., the different double curves. The four lines that lead off from the feather headdress symbolize the Earth and the four winds.

7

The Northeast

ALGONQUIN, DELAWARE, HURON,
ILLINOIS, IROQUOIS, MICMAC, MOHAWK,
ONEIDA, ONONDAGA, SENECA,
SHAWNEE, WINNEBAGO

nushinen Our father (who)	Wajok in heaven	ebin lives,	tchiptook may	delwigin your name
meguidedemek be respected	Wajok in heaven!	n'telidanen To us,	tchiptook may	ignemwiek be granted	ula you
nemulek to see	uledeehinen when you stay	Natel There	Wajok in heaven	deli as	ehkedoolk you are obeyed
tchiptook may (you)	deli thus	ehkedulek be obeyed		makimiguek on Earth	eimek. where we are.
Delamukubeniguai As you have given to us		eehemieguel just so	apeh also	negueeh now	kiehkook today
delamookteeh give	neguunenwin our food	nilunen to us.	deli abikchiktakaehik We forgive those	
wegalwinametnik who have hurt us		elp so	kel you	nixkam oh God	abikehiktwin forgive (us)	elweultiek our errors.
melkeninreeh Hold us tight	winnehudil with your hand (so that we)		mu don't	k'tygalinen fall,
keginukamkel keep us away from	winnehiguel suffering	twaktwin (and) evil.		N'delieteh. Amen.

Variation of the Lord's Prayer in pictorial Native American writing

Pictorial Writing of the Northern Tribes

A few Native American tribes of the Northern regions have, over time, developed structured pictorial writing. They include the Dakota, Hidutsa, Mandan, and some of the tribes of the Algonquin nation. The Micmac are part of the Algonquin nation and have created the rendering of the Lord's Prayer on the opposite page. This example shows that pictorial writing not only serves to record specific events, but it can also be used to express spiritual ideas—even translating concepts that are foreign to Native Americans, such as this text of Christian origin.

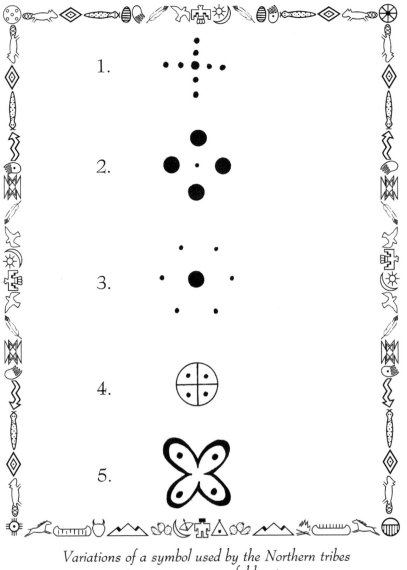

1.

2.

3.

4.

5.

*Variations of a symbol used by the Northern tribes
to ensure a successful hunt*

Symbols of the Highest God

The decorative arts of the North use, among others, a symbol of four dots surrounding a fifth dot (Fig. 2). Often, the symbol is reinforced by a cross and bound by a circle (Fig. 4). These patterns are common to the entire Northern hemisphere. They can mostly be found with the Naskapi as well as with the Southern Algonquin. In most cases, a mystic series of five dots was used to decorate the skins of hunted animals (Fig. 2), and sometimes the number of dots around a central point increases up to eight (Figs. 1 and 3). As a rule, Figure 1 marks a shaman's drum.

Figure 5 is a variation of the symbol and can be found in Labrador, the sea provinces, and Maine. It is put, for example, on playing pieces made of bone or on containers made of birch bark. Figure 2, however, is used by all hunters of the subarctic region to decorate drums, bowls, and rattles.

The dots describe a vision of sunbeams and personify *tchementu*, the highest being. Sunbeams coming through gaps in the cloud cover, brightly illuminating the otherwise dreary landscape, are regarded by the Naskapi hunter as a revelation of the Great Spirit. These phenomena represent the answer to the hunter's prayers. The Great Spirit blesses him with these patches of sunlight and shows him the hiding places of the deer. Red dots symbolize the patches of sunlight.

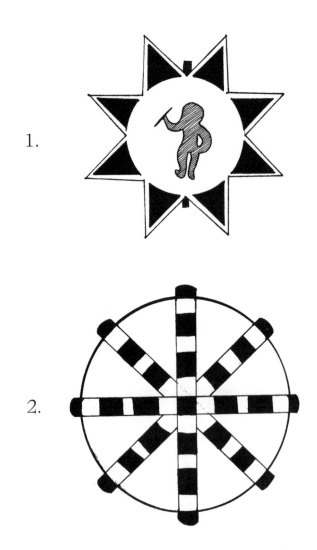

1.

2.

Protective cosmic dream badges of the Northern tribes

Dream Badges

It was and still is common in the tradition of the Northern tribes and the prairie Algonquin to record dream visions with drawings. The person who has the vision mainly uses mythical and non-naturalistic elements. Cosmic visions of the Earth, Sun, rainbows, and morning star are typical of tribes living in woodlands and of the prairie Algonquin, who brought this tradition with them from their Northern origin. In these motifs, people and animals are usually placed in the realm between the nighttime sky and the Earth, i.e., the cosmic realm. This can be seen in the tepee decorations of the Arapaho and the Algonquin Blackfoot.

Figure 1 shows the badge of the Sun dreamers of the Menomini. Although a Sun vision can be represented in the simplest ways—for example, with a circle surrounded by sunbeams—this emblem reveals an elaborate symbolic content. It is made up of a circle of eight triangles around a central figure with one arm lowered, which indicates the fall, and another arm raised, which points toward spring.

Figure 2 represents a dream badge with a protective function. These so-called *Päähra* were fashioned from birch bark by the Lenape tribe to be decorated and placed on a wampum chain. The plaque is divided into eight segments and worn near the chest or stomach. The Lenape also referred to it as an idol.

Dream renderings, such as this eight-pronged star, may also be counted as part of the motifs referring to the cardinal points. Badges like these are still common among the Central Algonquin and record a person's memories of visionary dreams.

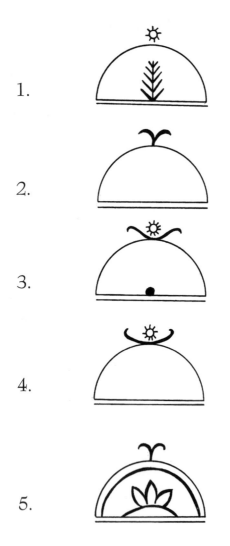

1.

2.

3.

4.

5.

Mythical representations of the sky by the Iroquois and the Algonquin

Symbols of the Light Tree

This decoration can be found mainly among the Iroquois, but it is also used by the Algonquin tribes. It is mostly found as an embroidery on the seams of clothes, on leggings, moccasins, tobacco pouches, and other objects.

According to the world-view of the Iroquois, the solid surface of the sky dome is inhabited by the *ongwe*, the original models of all beings on Earth. Since there is neither sunlight nor moonlight on that side of the sky, they receive all the light from the light tree and its flowers. In the same manner that the *ongwe* are a reflection of all living beings on Earth, the light tree is also represented on Earth by massive elms or pine trees.

This tree always divides the surface of the cosmos in two and embroideries show it either in a naturalistic manner (Fig. 1) or depicted by three leaves (Fig. 5) while the Sun shines down from above. Some drawings only show the light tree of the sky rooted in the surface of the sky dome (Fig. 2); others show it with the Sun in its branches (Figs. 3 and 4).

In some renderings, both trees actually unite to give the clearest testimony of the return of the *ongwe*-land to the lower world.

Myth of creation of the Onondaga, Iroquois, Seneca, and Mohawk

The Woman who Fell from the Sky

The picture on the opposite page represents the myth of creation as told by the Onondaga, Iroquois, Seneca, and Mohawk.

A young woman (at the top of the picture) was once accused of adultery by her much older husband. Even though she was pregnant, she was thrown out of the world above the sky dome. While she fell, a flock of ducks came to her aid and led her safely down to the water that stretched underneath the sky. In order to help her find a permanent home, the animals of the sea decided to dive for land. The turtle (at the center of the picture) agreed to carry the land on its back, whereupon the land started to spread and the turtle, too, increased in size until the Earth reached the size that it has now. At exactly that moment, the young woman who fell from the sky gave birth to a daughter.

Later, the daughter, who was impregnated by the wind, gave birth to twin sons. The first son is the hero of culture and is called "shoot" or "good thoughts" (on the left of the picture), whereas the second one is called "flintstone" or "evil thoughts" (on the right of the picture). The daughter dies giving birth to the second son so that her mother becomes the guardian of the twins. While "shoot" conducts the act of creation by making animals and plants, and trying to create an ideal world, "flintstone" tries to thwart his brother's plans and make life difficult for the people. He is aided by his grandmother, who made the Sun from the head of her dead daughter and hid it far in the East, until "shoot" stole it with the help of the animals and put it up in the sky.

Again and again, "flintstone" would hide the animals "shoot" created in a cave, and again and again, "shoot" would come and free them. Keeping the animals prisoner is symbolic of hibernation. After he has banished "flintstone," who in some versions of the legend becomes the ruler of the underworld, "shoot" finally retires from the Earth.

1.

2.

3.

4.

5.

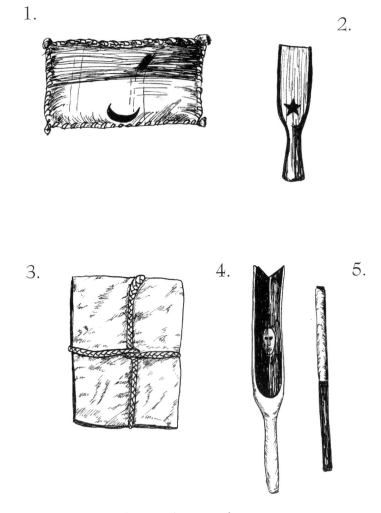

Shaman drums and accessories

Ceremonial Drums of the Lenape

Figure 1 shows the ceremonial drum of the Lenape *Smoothtown* ritual. The shape of the drum indicates the number "four," which Native Americans hold sacred. Furthermore, it is painted in two different colors and decorated with a crescent Moon on the light-colored half.

Figure 2 shows one of the prayer sticks used in this ritual.

The drum in Figure 3 comes from New Fairfield and is about 17 inches long. The drumstick for this drum (Fig. 4) measures almost 19 inches long and has been carved with a human face.

Figure 5 shows another prayer stick belonging to the *Smoothtown* ritual, and like the drum, it is painted in two colors.

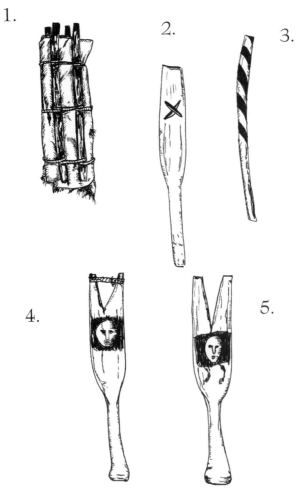

1.

2.

3.

4.

5.

Ritual objects

Ritual Objects of the Lenape

Figure 1 shows a drum that is made of dried deerskin. It is about 38 inches long and is used exclusively for religious ceremonies.

For the Northern tribes, the deer has the same significance that the buffalo has for the tribes of the Plains. It personifies the Earth.

The drumstick shown in Figure 2 was used during the first eight nights of the ceremony. Next to it, Figure 3 shows a prayer stick measuring almost 20 inches.

Figures 4 and 5 show drumsticks that were used after the eighth night. Figure 4 has the carved face of a man, while Figure 5 shows the face of a woman.

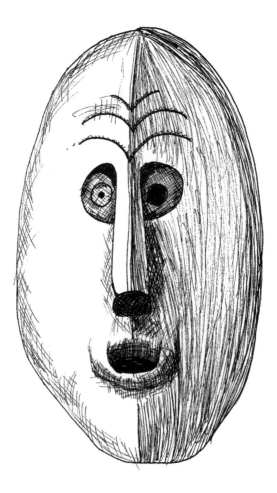

The keeper of wild animals

The Wooden Misinghalikun Mask

The Lenape carved this *misinghalikun* mask from wood and painted it half red, half black. This so-called "solid living" face measures 13 inches long. During the yearly ceremony, the mask-bearer also carries a stick, rattle, and bear skin pouch, while his body is covered with a dark bear skin.

The *misinghalikun* is revered by the Unami-Lenape in Oklahoma. According to their beliefs, it watches over all wild animals and can sometimes be seen riding a deer or watching over it. It lives in the Rocky Mountains and was given its job by god himself. Its appearance during the yearly ceremony has no doubt something to do with its rule over the deer.

The Menomini cosmos

Menomini Leather Shield

The drawing on the opposite page describes the Menomini cosmos. The decoration on this deerskin blanket goes back to a revelation in a dream and documents the beginning of bundle painting.

There are four layers that tower above the Earth. First, above the realm of the people, there are the birds that fly low and the bald-headed eagles. In the second layer, there are the swans and the golden eagles—birds that fly higher. In the third layer of the sky live the thunderers. In the fourth and uppermost layer resides the great god *Mätsch Häwätuk*.

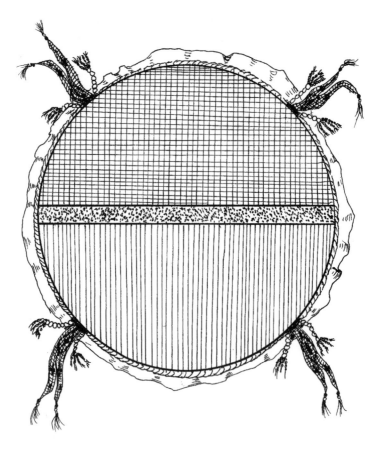

The drum as a symbol of the highest being

The Painting of the Dream Dance Drum

Around the year 1880, the Menomini-Ojibwa suddenly developed the dream dance. Central to this new ritual was a giant dream dance drum on which the attention of the tribe was focused from then on.

The drum was made from an enormous washing bowl and regarded as the direct embodiment of the Great Spirit itself. Bead-embroidered ribbons were attached to the four cardinal points at the edge of the drum to form the hands and feet of the highest being. The cylindrical body stands for the body of the highest *manitu*. The drum skin was painted with cosmic patterns: in the middle was the yellow path of the Sun (dotted), above it rose the blue of the Northern sky (grid pattern), and below it showed the red of the Southern sky (vertical hatching). Therefore, the body of the great *manitu* mirrored the world. Mythology often equates the drum with the highest being.

Giant bird of the Illinois

Rock Painting of the Illinois

The Illinois once painted the picture of the *piasa* onto a rock above a river near Alton, Illinois. Missionaries discovered it in the 17th century.

The *piasa* was a bird-like creature with scales on its body, a long tail, antler-like horns, and red eyes. This legendary bird was said to appear once a year on the first day of fall at sundown. This is when it would be seen gliding above the river in search of a home for the winter.

According to the legend, the Illinois were tormented by this bird for so long that finally their great chief Ouatogo, acting as bait, stood up to the creature. At the same time, twenty of his warriors ambushed and killed the monster with their bows and arrows. The chief remained unharmed.

As a reminder of this event, the Illinois created this rock painting. Whenever they passed it in their canoes, they would shoot at it- first, with fire arrows, then with rifles.

8
The Totem Animals

According to Native American tradition, each person is connected with nine animals that will accompany him on his path through life and nurture his talents and abilities. Each animal teaches the wisdom of one of the seven directions: East, West, North, South, up, down, and inside. In addition, there are the two escorts on the left and right who have been visiting us in our dreams for a long time.

If you would like to know which are your totem animals, you can find out with the help of an oracle. Write the names of all the totem animals on pieces of paper, lay them out face down, and then pick out nine with your left hand. If you feel an affinity to animals from other continents or cultures that are apart from the typical totem animals in the next several pages, you can add their names as well.

Since all living beings are linked by a creative force, or the Great Spirit, it is possible to invoke the animals directly. This requires an attitude of respect and the willingness to accept help. The relationship is formed by concentrating on a particular animal and the desire to establish contact with its powers.

To describe the many, often complicated totem rituals would go beyond the scope of this book, particularly since they differ significantly from tribe to tribe.

If you decide to work with totem animals, you could even develop your own rituals, ensuring only that the procedure makes sense to you and that you have incorporated the typical characteristics of the animal.

The Weasel

The weasel looks behind the scenes and recognizes all the little details that lead to a great event. For this reason, it was very common for kings in the past to wear garments made of ermine or weasel fur. People who possess the powers of the weasel are often underestimated, since their sense of discretion does not allow them to reveal their insights. In the business world, they are usually without match, since their acute powers of observation always render their competitors' intentions transparent.

Nevertheless, the weasel is a difficult power totem. Often, those who have the powers of the weasel feel a degree of responsibility for what they notice about others. Many just want to be left in peace, and some even want to lead the life of a hermit because, in the end, knowing too much can make a person lonely and can become a real burden.

You can invoke the powers of the weasel to discover the background to a problem.

The Porcupine

In the medicine wheel, the porcupine takes the place of an innocent child. Its disposition is friendly and loving; it is never the instigator of trouble. If it happens to be attacked by another animal, which rarely occurs, its spines will protect it.

The teaching of the porcupine embraces faith and trust. Since faith is said to move mountains, this is a very significant power to have. This animal teaches us to be open, to discover new miracles every day, and to free ourselves from the serious and routine world of adults. The porcupine has held on to a child-like sense of wonder and its trust in the divine plan where everything will turn out all right. Its friendliness and openness unlock the hearts of others in order to share love and joy.

The Eagle

The eagle personifies the divine power. It can rise high in the sky, higher than any other living being, and, thus, comes close to the Great Spirit. Rising to such heights, it can observe life in its entirety.

The eagle teaches the importance of recognizing the whole pattern of life with its bright and dark sides. This means we should regard both positive and negative events as experiences that can serve a higher purpose and help to develop the self. The power of the eagle, therefore, requires trust in divine leadership and only by examining his strength of soul can a person acquire the power of the eagle.

Eagles' feathers have been used by shamans since ancient times to heal the aura of the sick. The message of the eagle is: Defeat your fears and see beyond your horizon, become one with the element of air and fly!

The Falcon

The falcon is the messenger among the animals; it is roughly comparable to the divine messenger in Greek mythology. The cry of the falcon always announces a special event, which may be associated with joy as well as with danger. It is important to observe the present situation closely and, if necessary, take the initiative and act courageously.

The message of the falcon also says to reach out and accept the gifts of the Great Spirit, which are there but may not yet have been noticed. People who have the power of the falcon are keen observers, who do not miss the smallest detail nor lose sight of the whole. They recognize the signs and receive advice from the other worlds.

Whenever you hear the piercing cry of the falcon, take note! Aim for a better perspective to be able to interpret the message from the falcon.

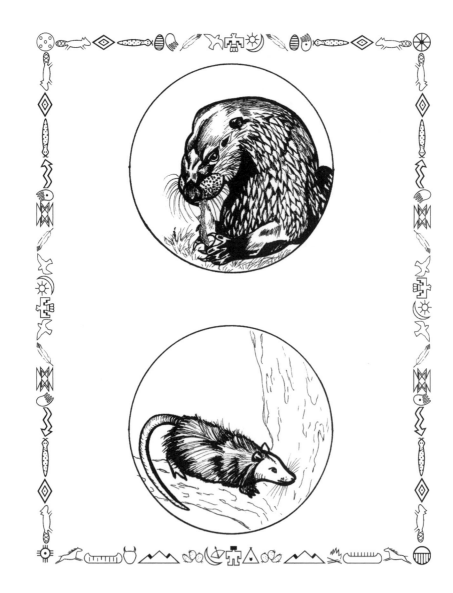

The Otter

The otter stands for the female energy. Its elements, water and Earth, are also those of woman. Its balancing power enables the otter to play and have fun with its offspring all day. The otter would never start a fight, because it does not know aggression and imbalance. Therefore, it approaches everybody with curiosity and friendliness. It will only defend itself if attacked first.

Its physical shape also corresponds to the Native American image of femininity. It is slender and full of graceful coquetry. It teaches that being a woman is not equivalent with jealousy or envy, but means spreading joy and openness. It is the power of sharing kindness. People with the energy of the otter practice free love without control and power games. They float with the stream of life without tying themselves to material goods. This is the powerful, receiving-energy of women.

The Opossum

The opossum is the digression expert in the animal kingdom. If all of its strategies fail, it pretends to be dead. Most of the time, the confused hunter will turn away, thinking the hunt is over. Even though the opossum could use its claws and teeth to defend itself, it rarely does so. In addition to the visible masquerade, it can produce a slightly sweet scent of death, which further confuses its adversaries.

The opossum teaches to use one's intellect and intuition to find the way out of tricky situations. An attacker will lose interest if the victim pretends to be dead by feigning indifference and not even showing if it is injured. The warrior can also utilize the power of the opossum when he faces a seemingly superior opponent by making sure to surprise and confuse him. Victory ultimately depends on the right strategy.

The Butterfly

The butterfly symbolizes transformation into something higher. It teaches us to make conscious changes to our lives, create new conditions, and make dreams come true.

Every new idea and every step toward self-fulfillment reflect the development of the butterfly. The egg of a butterfly signals the birth of a new idea. The larvae stage stands for the time when one should decide whether or not to put this new idea into practice. The cocoon represents an inward journey to establish a connection between the idea and oneself. Finally, the hatching of the butterfly symbolizes the beginning of a new reality. The joy of the new creation may now be shared with others.

These four steps of transformation are continuously taking place in our lives and are necessary for our development.

The attributes of the butterfly help to arrange one's thoughts and to consciously take the next step.

The Dragonfly

The dragonfly, creature of the winds, represents the tricking of the senses and change. Its iridescent wings are reminiscent of magical times and, thus, let us realize that there is only seeming reality in this world.

The dragonfly teaches that nothing is quite the way it seems, and that it is therefore necessary not to allow our senses to be tricked. Furthermore, the dragonfly conveys messages from elementary beings and plant spirits.

If you wish to make changes, call to the energy of the dragonfly.

The Moose

The power of the moose lies in self-respect. Its pride and strength are extremely impressive. The moose teaches that one should visibly express joy over a successful achievement, just like the moose bellowing loudly during the rutting season. The aim is not to ask for recognition, but to give expression to happiness. Others will be swept along with such an enjoyment of success.

Elders often possess the power of the moose. They can encourage and instruct the younger people to use courage wisely and achieve success. They know when it is best to be friendly and when one should voice one's anger. The moose shows how important it is to give yourself a pat on the back and respect what you have achieved. Likewise, you should give praise and encouragement to everybody else involved, because it is important for everybody to receive encouragement.

The Buffalo

The buffalo stands for affluence. If a white buffalo, the holiest of animals, appears, it is a sign that prayers have been heard and that a period of wealth is about to begin.

In legends, it was the "White Buffalo Calf Woman" who brought the people the holy medicine pipe. Its tobacco united all forces of nature and its smoke rose as a visible prayer. The particles suspended in the smoke made it possible for the spiritual beings to grant wishes.

The buffalo teaches that everything exists in abundance if it is respected and accepted with gratitude. It is important to praise all gifts that are received and also to pray for the divine wealth being granted to others. The buffalo also points out that goals can only be reached with the power of the Great Spirit.

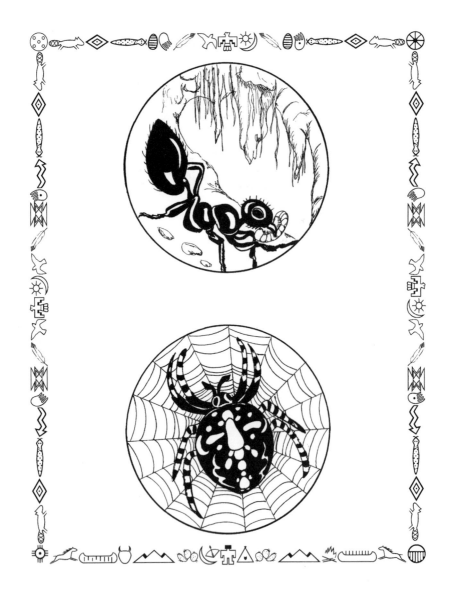

The Ant

The ant is tenacious, strong, aggressive, generous, and very meticulous. Its most pronounced characteristic, however, is patience. An ant can wait patiently for hours, hidden in the sand, for its prey, or it can transport larger items over long distances without giving up. Ants typically live in groups, and everything is done for the ant colony and the good of the community.

The ant teaches that you will have everything you need and will receive it when you need it most. It is the symbol of basic trust. It knows that it will ultimately be rewarded for all its efforts. If your activities are for the common good, then you will receive back any energy that you have expended. It may be, however, that you will have to put greater effort into the realization of your dreams and use your creativity.

The Spider

The shape of the spider and the number of its legs both show the number "eight," which represents infinity. The spider embodies the unlimited number of possibilities within creation. Doubling the number "four" indicates both the four winds and the four cardinal points.

The spider instructs us to accept responsibility for anything that happens in our lives. We weave the web of our destiny. The victims who become caught in the web have not yet understood this lesson and have become entangled in a reality that appears to be unchangeable.

The spider teaches that each being is responsible for its own plan of life. It is important not to lose oneself in deceptions of the senses, and it is helpful to write down one's progress to remember how certain strategies have led to success. The spider also stands for the development of writing.

The Horse

The horse shows both earthly strength and unearthly powers. It is regarded highly throughout the world and connected with the magical powers of shamans. With the help of the horse's speed, a person can cover long distances in a relatively short period of time. The horse has also made transportation of goods a lot easier. It is, therefore, the first and foremost totem animal of civilization. The power of an engine to this day is measured in horsepower.

Riding a horse conveys a sense of freedom. It teaches that power cannot be attained by force, but rather that it is given to him who is willing to accept responsibility in a respectful manner. Just as the horse carries its rider on its back, the rider carries responsibility for everything around him. The power of the horse is the wisdom to remember all the steps in one's life and learn from them. This includes experiences from a previous life. Real power is strength used with wisdom. This requires love, compassion, and the willingness to share one's achievements and insights with others. It is important not to let our ego deny us access to this power.

The Antelope

The antelope's message is to act sensibly. It knows about the cycles of life and the mysteries of life and death. This is why it can act fearlessly and realistically. Medicine men strive for the power of the antelope.

The antelope always pursues a higher objective with its actions that will benefit the community. If you happen to be entangled in a difficult situation, call to the power of the antelope, pay attention to the message you receive, and then act. The antelope will advise you to trust in your intuition and own strength. Whenever you feel the need to take a leap forward, pluck up your courage and do it.

The Badger

The badger teaches how to deal with power creatively and successfully. Most animals avoid contact with the badger, for despite its small stature, the badger makes a dangerous adversary. Its aggressiveness and wildness make it unpopular with others. The badger is the totem animal of powerful healers and medicine women. People who possess the power of the badger can use its tenacity very effectively to heal. They will never give up until they ultimately defeat the disease.

The badger teaches to use one's anger in order to change unacceptable circumstances in life. Shrug off your lethargy and take action! Use the energy of the attack to propel yourself forward, but do not run everybody into the ground in the process. Always pay attention to your inner balance.

Badger-people are often the boss who is feared by many, but who keeps everything going in the end. If he is in a bad mood, he can be cold and mean. His strength lies in showing his feelings without worrying about the reaction of others. There is no place for panic for a badger-person; he always keeps a cool head even in difficult situations.

The Hare

The hare represents fear. Its constant terror of being killed and devoured by a larger animal means that it attracts these animals almost magically, and that what it fears most will certainly come to pass.

What you expect usually happens in this world, and the hare, therefore, teaches that what you fear the most will most likely happen. Try not to worry that you might be struck by illness or some other misfortune, because otherwise you will just attract such events. This is proof of the universal law that you are always the cause of what happens to you.

The Frog

The frog is linked to the element of water and the cleansing powers of rain. It is associated with all rites of initiation connected with water. Just as a human being learns about the element of water first in the mother's womb, the frog spends its early life in the water as a tadpole. It has the power to summon rain by singing a certain song.

People who possess the power of the frog are often good mediums or healers. This power enables them to cleanse their environment from any negative influences, and it is used to rid haunted places of ghosts or cure the sick from their illnesses. The frog is always the messenger announcing the start of a new life.

If the frog leaps into your dreams, it may be time for you to take a break, pay more attention to yourself, and cleanse yourself. This includes freeing yourself from circumstances in your life that are unpleasant and a burden. It is important to create a space for a new life.

The Lizard

The lizard symbolizes the dream world beyond time and space. It dreams of the future. The lizard teaches how to use dreams to create a future reality. Since it can see into the future, it always knows in advance what will happen. This includes self-fulfilling prophecies. One dreams of a situation, and then it is up to the dreamer to decide whether to continue fueling this situation and, thus, make it real or not.

The lizard encourages you to look more closely at your dreams and your shadow in detail. Have you seen your future, your hopes, or your fears? The teaching holds that you are responsible for every single event in your life, consciously or not, because everything that happens springs from your wishes and fears.

The Bear

The bear embodies self-observation, because every winter, it retires to a cave to reflect on the events of the past year. It enters into the great silence, the big empty, to find the answers to all questions.

Many people also choose the path of silence and solitude to find themselves. This is an opportunity to obtain answers, since all the answers can be found within ourselves. Self-observation is necessary to recognize one's wishes. The power of the bear embraces this receiving, female energy. The bear withdraws into a dream world every winter on the search for answers and is reborn every spring.

The bear teaches how important it is to recognize the right time to take a step back from the noisy world around us and from our thoughts. For it is in silence that we can hear the voice of the higher self that knows the answers to all questions and holds the solution to all problems. Use the power of the bear to realize your goals.

The Wolf

The wolf is associated with the star Sirius in the constellation Canis Major, from which, according to ancient legends, the teachers of old originated. Hence, the wolf is a teacher that returns to its pack after extensive forage to tell everyone about new observations and experiences. It lives in a close-knit family circle without sacrificing its independence. It chooses a partner to whom it is faithful throughout its life. When the wolf howls at the Moon, it identifies with its power, its spiritual energy, and the unconscious through which all knowledge can be accessed.

The wolf can give you the power to become a teacher for others to understand life better and find their own path. The wolf energy will also enable you to establish a connection with your own inner leader.

The Hummingbird

The hummingbird loves life and happiness. It enjoys the beauty of the flowers and the harmony of nature. It is sensitive to disharmonious vibrations, which may cause it to take flight. Its medicine is to spread love and happiness among the flowers, animals, and people. Many plants live and flower for the hummingbird, because it is responsible for their propagation by collecting their nectar.

The magic of the hummingbird lies in being able to open hearts. Its feathers are, therefore, often used in love spells. Its flight technique is unique among birds, as it can fly forwards, backwards, and hover in one spot. According to old Mayan teachings, it already belongs to the next cultural era, the fifth world. This tiny, fragile bird does not understand worldly concerns; its life is one big journey of happiness.

People who have the energy of the hummingbird display similar characteristics. They are constantly searching for balance and joy, helping others to enjoy life, and bringing forth the best from everybody. Like the hummingbird, they despise ugliness and discord and will always find places where beauty resides.

The Swan

The power of the swan lies in accepting the gift of change. As the swan submits to the higher plan of the Great Spirit, it evolves from the "ugly duckling" in its youth to a graceful adult swan. Since it is willing to accept this gift, it is allowed to see into dreams.

People with its power can see into the future, because they are willing to let the plan of divine power materialize. The swan teaches to bring consciousness into balance with all levels of being and develop one's intuition. It is important to admit to the ability of knowing about the future.

The Mouse

The mouse examines everything very closely. It is the most pedantic of all the animals. It encourages us to take a closer look and to establish a system for everything we know. It, therefore, embodies today's age of specialization, because it knows that it can always learn more and become more deeply involved. The other side of the coin is that the simplest things and processes are made complicated. By dissecting everything, one fails to see the whole; by examining things too closely, one loses sight of the context.

The mouse also possesses a very acute sense of danger. Since it is food for so many animals, it recognizes danger very early on and knows very well how to take shelter. Mouse-people are usually quite fearful, careful, and extremely diligent. Everything they do is well organized and systematic. It is important that they venture into the unknown, take a look at the enormousness of the universe, and practice tolerance. The medicine of the mouse teaches that it is important to examine things closely and react very quickly.

The Squirrel

The squirrel is a gatherer, building up stores so that it is prepared for anything unexpected. By hiding its food reserves in different places, it can survive even the longest winter. Its other characteristics are adaptability and speed. Its ploys to deceive and distract are unique. People with the energy of the squirrel find it difficult to sit still for one moment or to listen to others.

Seeing a squirrel in your dreams is a hint to prepare for the future, gather your strength, and brace yourself for significant changes. This also means to get rid of any "garbage" that will not come to anything anyway.

The Bat

The bat is the symbol of rebirth. On the one hand, bats live in dark caves that are reminiscent of the darkness of the grave; on the other hand, they rest with their heads down, which corresponds to the position of a baby just before it is born.

First and foremost, the bat explains the symbolic death, which a shaman has to die during his initiation. The fundamental idea is that the person undergoing the initiation has to face his fears and meet his real self to be able to discard his old ego and be reborn as a new person free from all restraints. Usually, the prospective shaman is subjected to merciless examinations, which will take him both to his mental and physical limits. It is quite common that the person to be initiated is buried in the Earth for a night.

If a bat flies through your dreams, this indicates that it is time to take leave of a part of yourself or a particular characteristic or circumstance. It is important to die a ritual death in order to then be able to develop further.

The Tortoise

The tortoise embodies Mother Earth. Its shell is its shield. Its slow gait is intended as a warning not to rush anything, but to wait for the right moment. Its eggs hatch because of the sunlight, and the tortoise thus points out how important it is to let one's ideas ripen in seclusion before sharing them with everybody.

The tortoise also teaches one to stand with both feet firmly on the ground connected with the Earth. Furthermore, it shows how to protect one's feelings and to withdraw into oneself. If it feels it is under too much pressure, it may even snap at and bite the encroacher.

261

The Roe Deer

The roe deer stands for unconditional love and kindness. Its speckled coat indicates that it does not make a distinction between light and dark, good and evil. The force of its love can heal the wounds of others regardless of how far they have wandered to the dark side.

If the roe deer appears to you in your dreams, it wants to point out how important it is to love others for what they are and, thus, to accept their weaknesses. Any kind of obsessive expectation should be discarded, because no one can be forced to change. Only the warmth of the heart can mend strained relationships and heal old wounds.

The roe deer also teaches that one should always maintain a positive attitude and look for the good without letting negative situations or people influence us. If you manage to remain friendly and confident even under the most adverse of circumstances, these circumstances will not linger for long and the path toward divine energy will be cleared.

The Dog

The dog is associated with faith and reliability. Its basic instinct is to serve its master, and even though it is often mistreated, it always answers with love. Since the dog strives to be respected by its master, it is, of course, possible to spoil it with the wrong training. Ultimately, the dog is the guardian of its master and willing to do anything for him, possibly even follow him into death. Traditionally, the dog is also the guardian of secret areas and ancient knowledge.

The dog's heart is filled with compassion, and it is willing to overlook human weakness. The dog can help bring these qualities to life in a person. It also teaches one to examine one's loyalty toward oneself and others.

The Lynx

The lynx is the bearer of secrets. It knows all the old secrets that have been forgotten a long time ago. It moves freely through space and time. Since it maintains silence most of the time, it is difficult to learn the things that it knows. Seeing a lynx in your dreams is a hint that there may be secrets within you or others of which you do not know.

If the power of the lynx is strong in a person, that person will have a very particular kind of perceptiveness. By using introspection, he will recognize the true selves of others along with his own identity. He will also discover the daily ritual of self-deception. The only way to glean some knowledge from the lynx is to pay it for revealing its wisdom, as is the custom with soothsayers and Native American medicine men based on the principle of exchanging energies.

The Fox

The most prominent characteristic of the fox is its ability to become one with its environment. Its brown summer coat helps render it invisible in the forest while its white wintry coat allows it to blend in with the snow. The fox is a very observant and fast animal, ready to take action at any time. Its power lies in its cleverness—for example, when leading its enemies astray. Another characteristic is its concern for its family. People who possess the power of the fox are usually quiet observers and are skilled at remaining unnoticed. This means that they blend into their environment, moving around unnoticed in any kind of company and society. They are masters of camouflage.

The fox teaches how to grasp the concept of unity and how to use this knowledge wisely on all levels. A fox charm is suitable mainly for those who travel a lot.

The Beaver

The beaver teaches industry and a sense of community; it is the ultimate master builder. The power of the beaver helps to realize ideas and dreams while working with others at the same time, because the beaver has a strong sense of family. It is always ready to defend itself; after all, it can fell entire trees with its teeth. This indicates the necessity of protecting what one has created and to always be vigilant.

You may call to the beaver to find a solution to a problem, as the beaver also advises one to keep one's options open. Its lodges always have several exits, which follows the motto that if one door is closed, another one will be open. Nobody should put restrictions on one's own opportunities. Whenever the beaver appears in your dreams, this may be a hint to put an old dream into practice or to finish off a project.

The Armadillo

The shell of the armadillo gives it optimum protection against the attacks of its enemies. It teaches humans to determine their own boundaries and to decide which experiences to allow in their lives.

The armadillo is the totem animal of medicine shields. Such a shield shows everything that its bearer wishes for or that describes him personally. Thus, everybody who encounters him will know, consciously or subconsciously, whom they have met and what his expectations are.

With its shell, the power of the armadillo prevents us from doing things that we don't really want to do, and it helps us to distance ourselves from the demands of others. It can help us to discard the old habit of saying "yes" to everything and it teaches us to recognize whether or not the circumstances that we are experiencing are of benefit to us.

267

The Coyote

The coyote is a mischievous but sacred rascal. It keeps busy constantly by trying to trick itself and others. Again and again, it becomes caught in its own trap, but it always manages to go free unharmed. Since it never learns from its mistakes, it continues to end up in the most awkward situations and, only because it is so adept at making the best of a bad situation, it never suffers any serious damage.

If you happen to have the power of the coyote, you will always act the clown and find yourself, seemingly through no fault of your own, in the strangest and most difficult situations. In these situations, it is important to still be able to have a laugh at your own expense; this is the only way for you to win the game after all.

The coyote presents us with a mirror and draws our own follies to our attention. No other animal has quite the ability of the coyote to stir up a repressed and serious society with elegance and carefreeness.

The Skunk

The skunk displays a healthy self-confidence. Its behavior is characteristic of the quiet self-assuredness of somebody who is aware of his own strength and power. Even though it does not have a dangerous weapon, it commands respect, because it threatens the sense of smell.

People who possess the power of the skunk usually have great charisma. They attract people with similar energies, just as the skunk smell is attractive to other skunks.

This small animal can teach us to accept ourselves completely and to develop a healthy pride. Since our views are always reflected in our attitude, we will automatically attract like-minded people and repel those who are not compatible or who simply wish to exploit us.

The Elk

The elk belongs to the largest species of deer. Apart from humans, its only enemy is the puma; it has to use all of its strength and endurance to escape from the puma. The strength of the elk lies in it knowing exactly what it can achieve and in using its strength to the optimum without overly exerting itself.

People who have the power of the elk attain their goals through perseverance and do not feel the need to always be among the first. It may be advantageous in a stressful situation to call on the power of the elk in order to recognize how to best utilize one's own energies, and at the same time suffering as little harm as possible.

The elk also stands for brotherhood among those of the same sex. This kind of support can be very encouraging and constructive through the exchange of similar ideas and experiences.

The Puma

The puma, or mountain lion, embodies pure power. This can be used in a positive manner, as seen with wise leaders, but it can also be abused. If you picture the perfect movements of this big cat, you can learn how to achieve a balance between body, mind, and soul.

The puma encourages us to stand by our convictions and always be truthful. These are the qualities of a true leader. However, there are certain disadvantages that come with being a leader. For example, it will be impossible to always please everybody and maintain peace. One also has to be careful not to be exploited by others. A person with the power of the puma must never be seen to be fearful or vulnerable, and has to be prepared to accept great responsibility. He also should keep a certain distance from other people.

The Turkey

The turkey represents the generosity of sharing and giving away; it sacrifices its own life so that others may live. The turkey teaches that it is not desirable to selfishly amass goods. On the contrary, it shows how important it is to share with others, to regard life as sacred, and, therefore, to ensure the welfare of others.

People who have the energy of the turkey always act with others in mind. This attitude does not spring from a false sense of guilt but comes from the realization that the Great Spirit lives in all beings. Additionally, there is the knowledge of the cosmic law that everything we give to others will one day come to back to ourselves.

The turkey teaches how to share. However, if it appears in your dreams, this may also mean that you are about to receive a gift or prize.

The Owl

The owl is symbolic of magic and second sight. It is often referred to as the eagle of the night. It can see extremely well in the dark night and its hearing is also very well developed. Its victims are unable to hear it approach, since the owl does not create any noise during flight.

People who possess the power of the owl are usually wizards or witches, or at least have a great interest in the occult. They are attracted either to white magic or, inadvisably, to black magic. It is almost impossible to keep a secret from an owl-person, as they see through even the best-hidden ploys. They always grasp the whole truth and often take this gift for granted. It is because of this ability that they are often unpopular and feared by others.

The owl is the essence of wisdom, since it can see and hear things that others cannot. It can help discover the truth and interpret signs of fate.

The Raven

The raven is regarded as the bearer of magic. It is the messenger from the great void beyond time and space, and the ether where everything originated and to where everything will return.

When a ceremony is held, the raven is always present to transport the energy of the message to its destiny. The raven's help makes it possible to heal people from a distance.

Those who have used black magic have good reason to fear the raven, because it throws back negative energies to where they originated.

The raven can help you to change your outlook and give you the courage to enter into the great secret. Look at its iridescent feathers and how they continuously change shape and color. See into the black emptiness to receive answers to your questions.

The Prairie Chicken

The prairie chicken symbolizes the sacred spiral of death and rebirth, the never-ending tunnel. Many tribes of the prairies venerate this bird with a dance that imitates the movement of a spiral. Somebody who is meditating can establish a direct link to the creator with the help of the energy of the prairie chicken.

The prairie chicken invites you to join it in dancing the dance of the sacred spiral in honor of the divine creation. It can help you to recognize how you move through spiritual and physical space and the effects your movements have. Compare the way in which you guide your energies with what you would like to achieve.

The Crow

The crow is the guardian of great secrets. It is the only creature with the ability to break the laws of this world by changing into other beings. It can also be in two places at the same time. The crow combines past, present, and future, because it lives in a void without any perception of time. Since it also combines light and shadow, it perceives its outer and inner truths simultaneously. The crow guards the sacred laws that came directly from god and proclaimed once that everything that exists is born by woman. The sacred law is the law of truth and must not be confused with the commandments of humans or any religious systems.

People who have the power of the crow must stand by their own realizations and constantly strive to live the truth that they discovered. Let your own higher self become your leader; change your shape and become your future self! Accept that the physical laws no longer apply and venture fearlessly into the future.

The Snake

By shedding its skin, the snake symbolizes change in the cycle of birth, life, death, and rebirth. It counts among its strengths the power of creation, of sexuality, of the soul, as well as of transformation and immortality. Snake-people are rare, because as part of their experiences they have to have come into contact with poison and have been able to transform the poison in their bodies into something harmless.

The snake belongs to the element of fire, which causes desire and passion in the physical realm and, in the spiritual realm, creates a connection with the Great Spirit and leads to all-encompassing wisdom.

Whenever the snake appears in your dreams, it is a sign of change as you come ever closer to perfection.

The Whale

The whale is the keeper of the Earth's history and secrets. It keeps alive the memories of the legendary motherland of Mu, which was once located in the west of America and to which all Native American tribes trace back their origins. The whale was once the witness of the great disaster to which the motherland fell victim.

People who own the power of the whale are often very perceptive and can, with the help of this gift, access all the information that exists in the universe. They often have telepathic powers, but the source of their knowledge frequently remains unknown to them. It is only with time that they realize how to utilize their powers.

The whale teaches one to find and blend with one's own original sound, because it carries the history of all living beings. It shows that the right frequency can heal and, with the help of the whale, you can learn to connect with the ancient language that was used for communication before language in its current form was developed. The whale always guides the way to discovering the meaning of your own life.

The Dolphin

The dolphin teaches about breathing, which connects us with life and the vital energies. By changing one's breathing pattern, it is possible to establish links with other beings and other worlds, since breath connects us with the Great Spirit and its entire creation.

People with dolphin-energy can act as mediators between the people and the inhabitants of the dream world or the divine power. The dolphin teaches one to overcome obstacles easily and joyfully by changing one's rhythm and, thus, one's energy pattern. Create a link with the great star people. Free yourself from all burdens through conscious breathing.

9
The Language of the Stone People

The symbols shown in this chapter can be found on stones, the bodies of the stone people. The meaning of these symbols is the same for different tribes. Those in search of truth should look out for stones at the side of the path bearing such engravings to guide them. They reflect one's personality and can also contain warnings, which is why they may be used in an oracle.

According to legends, these symbols were burnt into the bodies of the stone people by lightning beings at the end of the third world. Their aim was to help the people of the fourth world, today's world, in their struggle to achieve perfection.

These symbols are the pictorial representation of the flow of energies and of energetic, cosmic issues. They can be used as an aid for meditation, to charge other objects with energy; they can be used as an oracle or one can just look for them on stone bodies.

These motifs of cosmic energy are very similar to runes used in pre-Christian Europe. Runes were linked to trees and usually made from wood. Since Native American culture maintains a stronger link to the Earth, stones are regarded as carriers and transmitters of cosmic energies.

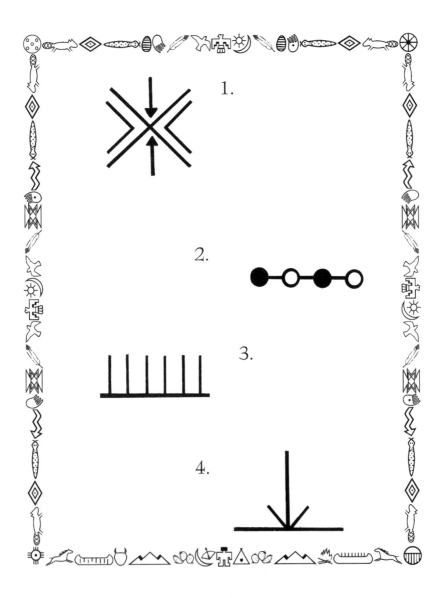

1.

2.

3.

4.

Symbols of Spiritual Energy

1. The large X, reinforced by two right angles in the East and the West and two arrows pointing to its center, is a symbol of *immortality*.

2. A line, which connects alternating dark and light circles, indicates the influence of *time*. In the oracle, it depends on the present situation whether the person concerned should take time, give time, or change a situation.

3. A horizontal line, which is met by several vertical lines, stands for *vitality* and the ability to make good use of it in the course of one's life.

4. The horizontal line, which is met by a downward-pointing arrow, symbolizes the power of *joy* necessary to overcome any suffering one has experienced.

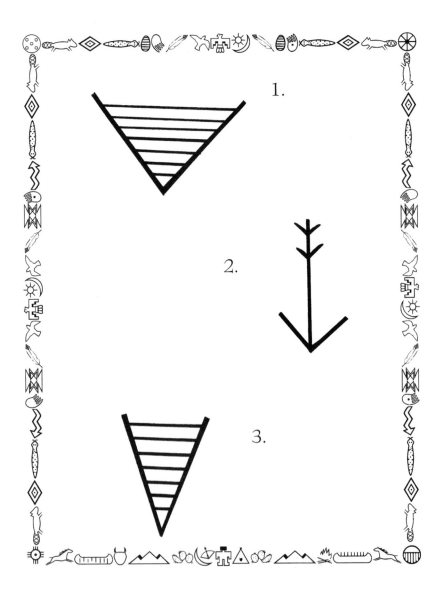

1.

2.

3.

Symbols of Spiritual Development

1. The wide V containing several horizontal lines indicates the development of existing talents. It is a symbol of *individual development*.

2. The downward-pointing arrow, which shows two small V's near the top end, indicates several existing *talents* that need to be developed. It is important to discover them and use them.

3. A narrow V containing several horizontal lines points to the ability to gather material or spiritual *wealth*. This inner and outer wealth already exists; it only needs to be made accessible.

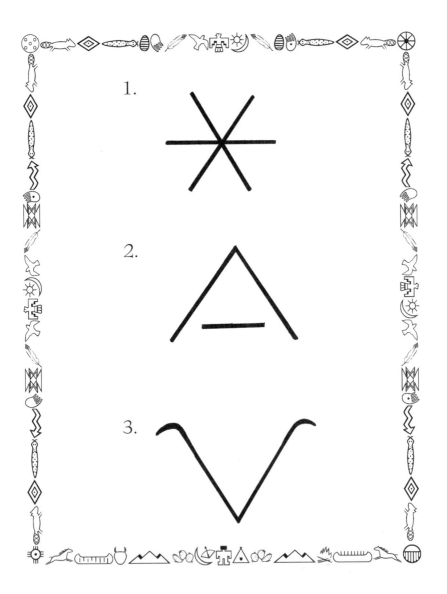

Symbols of Personality

1. The six-pronged star represents a great personality with a magnetic *aura*.

2. The upside-down V enclosing a horizontal line represents a quiet person who is a good *listener*. The line symbolizes a closed mouth.

3. The V with its ends bent outwards indicates a good and fair *judge*. The two ends show that this person is able to consider an argument or a situation from two different points of view.

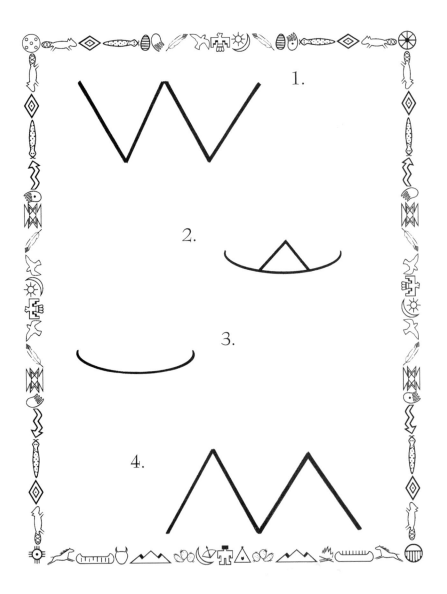

1.

2.

3.

4.

Symbols of Trust and Truth

1. Two linked V's stand for a person who is able to amalgamate two different points of view and is, thus, a good *diplomat*. If several V's are linked in this manner, this may indicate the combination of several positions and impressions.

2. When a wide U-shape meets an upside-down V, this indicates a truth-loving, *steadfast* individual. Because he always pays attention to the way others act, he is not easily deceived or fooled.

3. The wide U-shape on its own always refers to a positive person or somebody who lives the *truth*.

4. Two linked upside-down V's symbolize *self-confidence* and the strength to pursue one's own path and believe in one's intuition. This symbol can also frequently be found as continued zigzag lines in decorative Native American art.

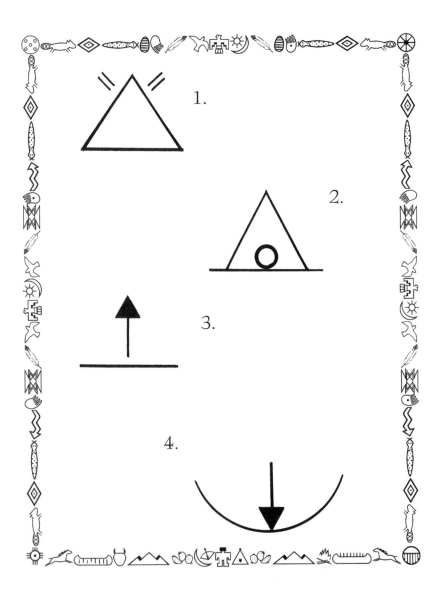

Symbols of Beauty and Learning

1. The morning star is represented by a triangle with two lines on either side at the top. It is the symbol of the *Beauty Way* and *Harmony Way*. It supplies the power and the talent to guide others onto this way by giving wise counsel.

2. A horizontal line on which an upside-down V stands enclosing a circle is symbolic of the *sense of taste*. It can help to live life more intensively and to get a taste for life, so to speak.

3. The symbol of *omnipresence* and of a keen sense of perception is represented by a horizontal line with an upward-pointing short arrow above it. This symbol may stand for a very attentive person, or it may point to the necessity to develop one's senses.

4. A downward-pointing arrow at the center of a curve indicates a *time of learning*. This symbol refers to the initiate who is prepared to walk the path of truth. It also strengthens the power of endurance.

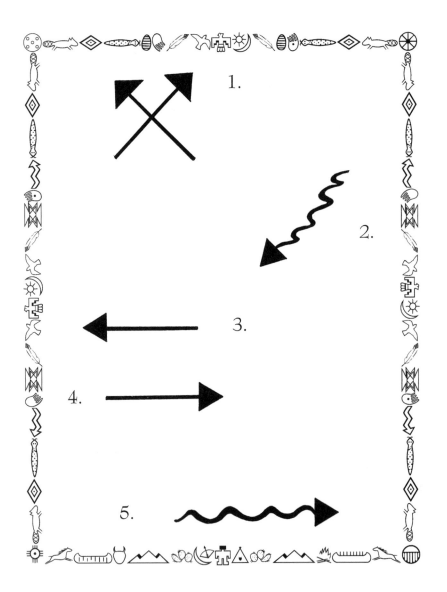

1.

2.

3.

4.

5.

Arrows

1. Two crossed arrows, both pointing upwards, are symbolic of a respectful *friendship*. The symbol also means that two people are willing to help each other.

2. A wavy line ending in an arrowhead symbolizes the energy of *wisdom*. If the head points down and to the left, this means that the person concerned mainly uses wisdom in his own life and has recognized his true self. If the head points down and to the right, this means a person who sees far and whose quiet powers of observation allow him to draw conclusions regarding future developments.

3. A horizontal arrow pointing to the left stands for the energy to *realize* wishes and ideas. As the arrow points to the left, it means that it is time to realize those wishes that have already gathered strength through repetition. It can point toward a time of taking action.

4. If the arrow points to the right, it stands for a growing potential of *creative power* and symbolizes future events. Intuition then enables us to move on to a new situation.

5. A wavy line with an arrowhead at its right end stands for an *acceleration* of all plans and developments that are currently significant.

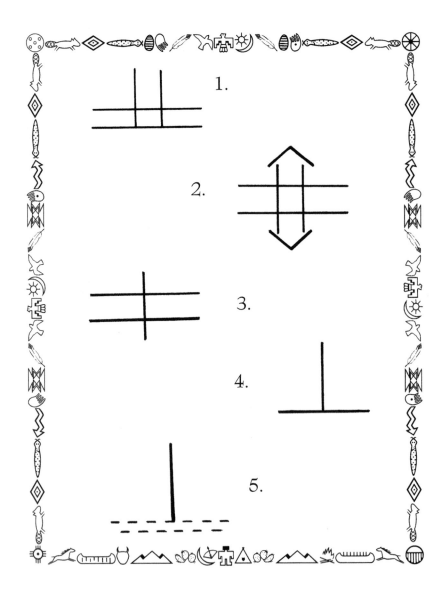

1.

2.

3.

4.

5.

Lines and Angles

1. The symbol of *health* consists of two horizontal lines crossed by two vertical lines that rest on the lower of the horizontal lines. This symbol shows the energies that enable the spirit to materialize on a worldly level and to maintain the body in which it has materialized. These are the energies that nourish and respect the body.

2. The energies, which give a direction and meaning to life, are symbolized by two horizontal lines crossing two vertical lines that have arrowheads at both ends. This is the symbol of *work* in the physical and spiritual sense.

3. If two parallel horizontal lines are crossed by a single vertical line, this stands for the power that enables a person to develop both physical and spiritual endurance. In the oracle, this can indicate a time when it is necessary to practice patience and perseverance.

4. If a vertical line is perpendicular to a horizontal line, this indicates that a *decision* on a particular matter has already been taken.

5. If the person concerned has yet to make a lot of decisions, this is indicated by a symbol in which the path of life (the vertical line) meets the path of the Earth, which is made up of several horizontal dashes.

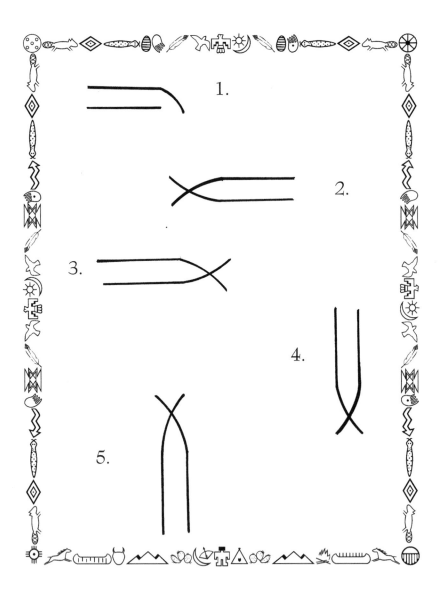

1.

2.

3.

4.

5.

Bent Lines

1. If the top of two parallel horizontal lines is bent down to the right at one end, this means with relation to the oracle that the person concerned needs the *encouragement* of others. It can also mean a lack of self-confidence.

2. Two parallel horizontal lines that merge on the left stand for a good family relationship. The symbol also refers to a person who likes to rely on the *family*.

3. This shows two horizontal lines merging on the right. The person concerned prefers to depend on others outside the family. The symbol can also refer to a person who is *gullible*.

4. Two parallel vertical lines that merge at the bottom are symbolic of *faith in one's own abilities*. They represent a person who relies solely on his or her own inner guidance.

5. Two parallel vertical lines merging at the top refer to a person with a mainly *spiritual outlook*. The person concerned trusts in a religious system. This may be the person's own religion or a foreign religious system.

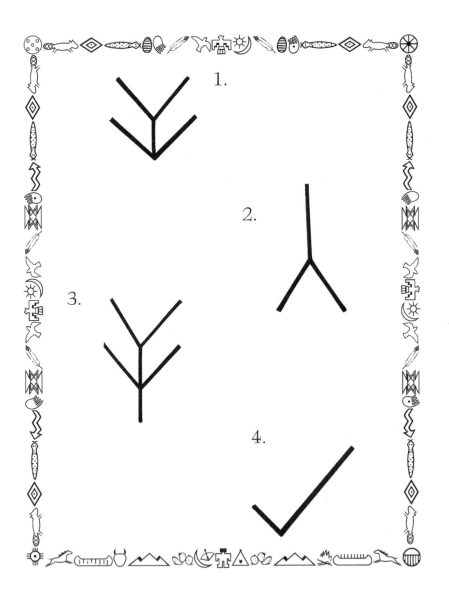

1.

2.

3.

4.

Angles and Lines

1. A vertical line that joins the middle of two V's form the symbol of *marriage*. It can also refer to any other form of lasting association.

2. A vertical line emanating from the apex of an upside-down V symbolizes spiritual powers that find expression in material objects. It is the symbol of *creative power*.

3. A vertical line that extends from the middle of two V's stands for creative ideas that are on the rise and refers to the *realization of these ideas* in life. It is also a symbol of truth.

4. The check mark stands for a person who is *open to new experiences*, willing to accept the ideas of others, and to try them out.

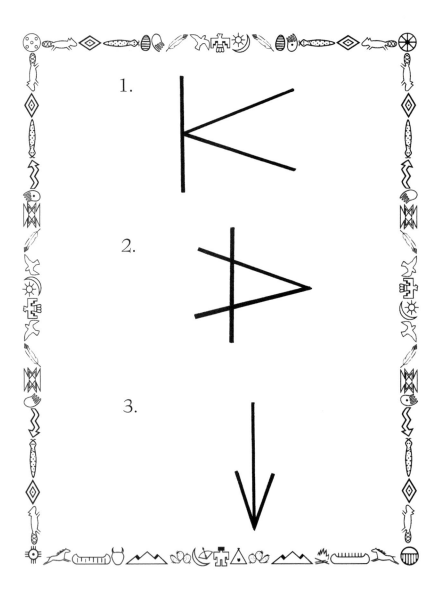

1.

2.

3.

Acute Angles Combined with Lines

1. This drawing shows the path of life (vertical line) touched by an acute angle. This indicates a *good habit* and encourages the person concerned to continue with his work and extend it.

2. An acute angle, which crosses the vertical line of the path of life, indicates that it is time to shed established customs, time to *change*, and start new projects. Only this will make growth possible.

3. The downward-pointing arrow stands for a spiritual person with *prophetic talents*.

1.

2.

3.

4.

5.

6.

Combined V Symbols

1. A W, or two linked V's, that stand on a horizontal line symbolize the *power of knowledge*. Using it will make life easier.

2. If several V's are connected on a horizontal line, they indicate the *path of learning*. The willingness to learn can suddenly open up a host of new opportunities.

3. Two upside-down V's, one above the other, stand for the *ambition* of a person to attain his goal and, thus, developing a strong inner creativity.

4. The symbol of *inner strength* consists of two V's placed on an upright rectangle. This symbol can help to develop courage and bravery.

5. A horizontal line met by a vertical line with a small V on both sides indicates a person who has the talent and wisdom to lead people. In the oracle, this may mean that one will become a leader or will be elected to a higher position.

6. An X with a horizontal line below it represents the symbol of *wise influence* designed to change things for the better. This energy must never be abused to gain control over others.

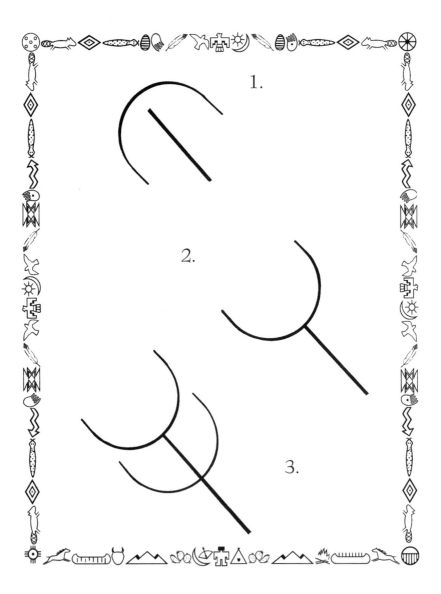

1.

2.

3.

Curves and Lines

1. A diagonal line pointing upwards but without touching the inside of a U carries the power of *compassion*. Thus, this sign can help to overcome prejudice.

2. A diagonal line connecting with the outside of a U can help to overcome one's own selfishness. The line, which refers to the self, divides at the end and continues in two directions. The symbol, therefore, contains the *energy of sharing*.

3. The symbol shown here reinforces the effect of Figure 2 through a second U intersecting the line. It is a symbol of *charity* to increase positive energies and spread joy and happiness. In the oracle, it can indicate that it is necessary to be charitable, or it can indicate a well-meaning person.

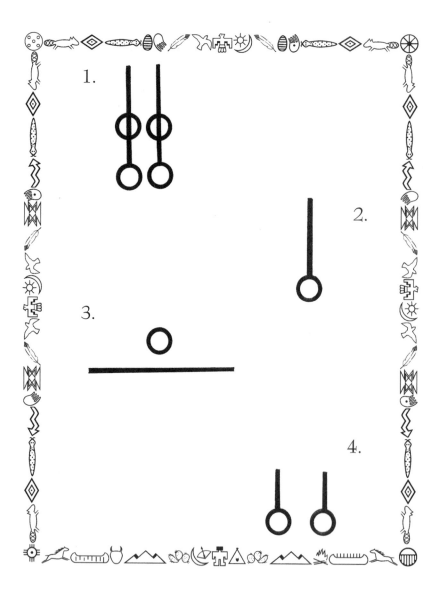

Small Circles and Lines

1. This drawing shows two vertical lines of equal length, dissecting two circles and ending on two circles. This is the symbol of *foreseeing the future*. This talent enables the strengthening of the energies of future events, thus, accelerating their realization. It also gives early warning of dangers and can help to avoid them.

2. A single vertical line ending on a circle stands for the positive, creative *power of the spirit*. It is the energy that affects the realization of an idea that will benefit everybody.

3. A horizontal line with a small circle above its center symbolizes the energy of sleep and *calmness*. Calm has its own power of enabling a person to recognize his inner voice. This symbol also stands for meditation.

4. Two short vertical lines, each ending on a small circle, stand for the *power of observation*. It is the symbol used to develop visual abilities.

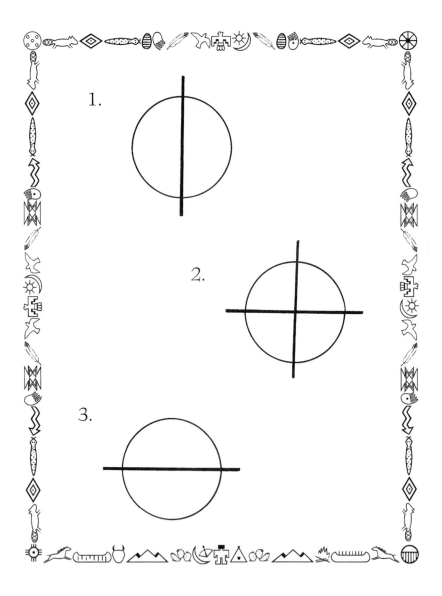

1.

2.

3.

Spiritual Circular Symbols

1. A vertical line dissecting a large circle stands for the power of *attraction* and the ability to use it wisely.

2. This figure shows the combination of a circle and a cross with its ends extending beyond the circle. It is symbolic of the four phases in the life of a human being: The age of learning (0–12 years), the age of accepting (12–24 years), the age of refining (24–36 years), and the age of wisdom (36 years and beyond). This symbol represents *change* and is similar in meaning to the European symbol of the wheel of life.

3. A horizontal line dissecting a large circle and extending beyond it on both sides represents growth and wealth that will be beneficial to a lot of people.

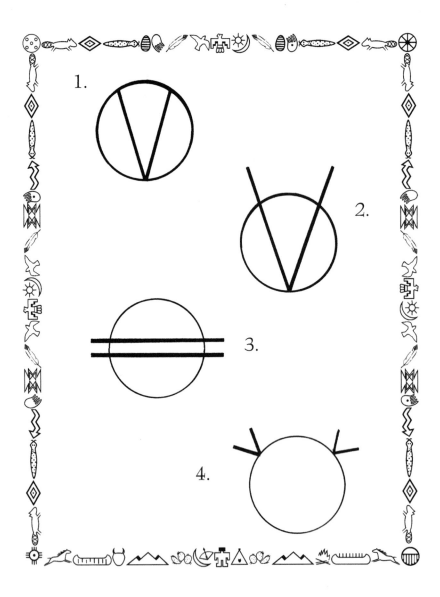

1.

2.

3.

4.

Angles, Lines, and Circles

1. A circle enclosing a V is regarded as a sign of *faith*. It attracts powers that make it possible to move mountains simply through faith in the divine power.

2. A circle whose enclosed V extends beyond it strengthens the energy of *patience* and perseverance. Both are necessary to achieve a deeper understanding of life and to understand the principle of cause and effect.

3. A circle that is dissected by two parallel horizontal lines is symbolic of *forgiveness*. This is necessary to overcome old relationships that only cause pain or in some way have a hampering effect on life. Through forgiveness, the person concerned liberates himself and the other person so that a new beginning is possible for both.

4. A circle with two small V's growing out of it symbolizes the *inner voice*. In this case, the circle represents the head and the two small V's represent the ears through which the inner voice is perceived. It is important to note that this symbol always refers to inner perception.

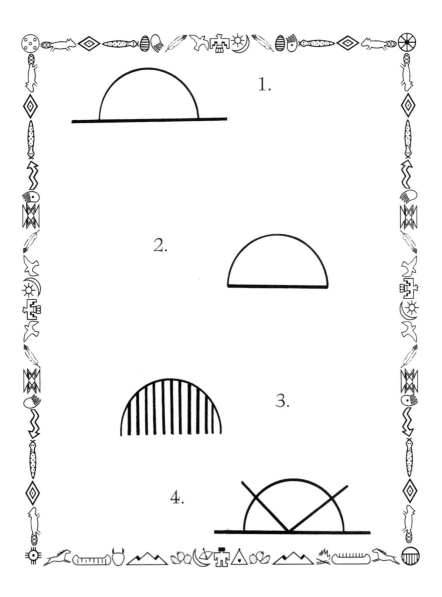

1.

2.

3.

4.

Combined Semi-circular Symbols

1. A semi-circle resting on a longer horizontal line symbolizes the dome of the sky. The horizontal line stands for the Earth. It is a symbol of stability and *reliability*. Whoever receives this sign in the oracle will have the ability to teach others self-confidence and to strengthen them.

2. A horizontal line connecting the ends of a semi-circle stands for the dome of the sky, representing a person's life from beginning to end. It contains the energy of *development*, which gives meaning to life. This symbol can encourage people to actively further their own development.

3. Several vertical lines below the arch of a semi-circle stand for life-giving rain. Thus, this is a symbol of fertility and growth with regard to material wealth and nourishment.

4. The symbol of all-embracing *healing* consists of a semi-circle and V resting on a longer horizontal line with the V extending beyond the semi-circle. This usually indicates a person with strong healing powers, or it can help to develop such powers.

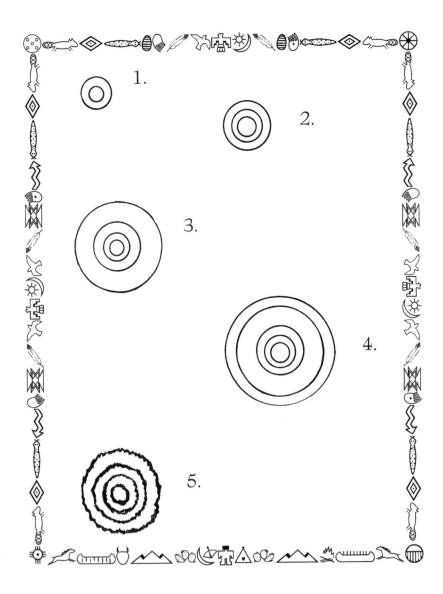

1.

2.

3.

4.

5.

Large Circles

1. Two concentric circles show a relationship between two people. This can refer to a *partnership* or to a member of the family.

2. If a third circle is added, this refers to the relationship with more distant *relatives*. It can, thus, refer to anybody bearing the same family name.

3. A fourth circle indicates a relationship with the plant world. It is also symbolic of the four *phases of life*.

4. A fifth circle represents the *environment*. In the oracle, it can refer to people either the person concerned works with or has a friendly relationship with. It can also refer to institutions.

5. Several concentric but irregularly-shaped circles, similar to the annual rings of a tree, always indicate *relationships*.

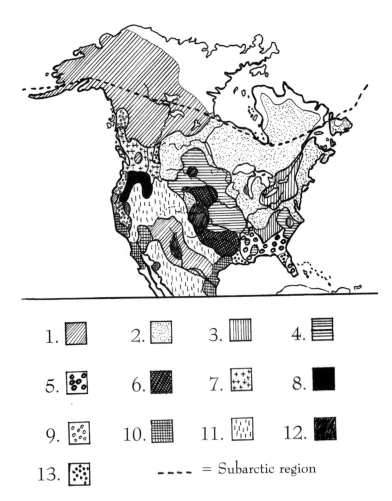

1. ▨   2. ⬚   3. ▥   4. ▤

5. ⬚   6. ◩   7. ⊞   8. ■

9. ⬚   10. ▦   11. ⬚   12. ◪

13. ⬚   ---- = Subarctic region

Nations and Tribes

1. Athabasca: Beaver, Tlingit, Haida, Chipewyan, Hupa, and Sarsee in the Northwest and in Alaska; Apache and Navajo in the Southwest.

2. Algonquin: Arapaho, Illinois, Blackfoot, Fox, Cheyenne, Cree, Delaware, Gros Ventres, Kickapoo, Menomini, Miami, Micmac, Mohican, Naskapi (Innu), Ojibwa (Chippewa), Ottawa, Penobscot, Piegan, Pawhatan, Sauk, Saulteaux, Shawnee, Winnebago, Yurok, and Blood.

3. Iroquois: Tuscarora, Seneca, Huron, Iroquois, Cherokee, Mohawk, Oneida, Onondaga, and Cayuga.

4. Sioux: Ponca, Otoe, Osage, Omaha, Minitari, Mandan, Crow, Iowa, Hidatsa, Assiniboin (Stoney), Dakota, Nakota, Oglala, and Chiwere.

5. Muscogee: Seminole, Natchez, Creek, Choctaw, and Chickasaw.

6. Caddo: Caddo, Arikara, Pawnee, and Wichita.

7. Mosan Tribes: Salish, Nootka, Flathead, and Kwakiutl.

8. Shahaptin: Nez Percé, Umatilla, and Yakima.

9. Penuti: Tsimshian, Maidu, Chinook, and Coos.

10. Hoka: Yuma, Pomo, Tonkawa, Mohave, Karuk, and Karankawa.

11. Uto-Aztecs: Ute, Hopi, Shoshone, Pima, Papago, Paiute, and Comanche.

12. Kiowa: Tano and Kiowa (Azteco-tanoic language family).

13. Isolated Tribes: Kutenai, Zuni, and Pueblo.

Index